W9-CHB-784

The
GOSPEL
of
JOHN

BIBLE STUDY

CORE CHRISTIANITY

The Gospel of John: Bible Study

© 2019 Core Christianity
1725 Bear Valley Parkway
Escondido, CA 92027

All rights reserved. No part of this book may be
reproduced or transmitted in any form or by any means,
electronic or mechanical, including photocopying,
recording, or by any information storage and retrieval system,
without permission in writing from the publisher.

Design and Creative Direction by Metaleap Creative
Cover Illustration by Peter Voth

Printed in the United States of America

First Printing — October 2019

CONTENTS

WHY
THIS
STUDY?

TO BEGIN, we would like to thank you, the students, congregants, church leaders, elders, pastors, and churches for supporting and using The Gospel of John. We hope it enriches your Christian life, challenges your heart, and builds up your faith to the glory of God.

This study was designed with several things in mind.

FIRST, WE DESIGNED THIS STUDY TO ADVANCE THE GOSPEL.

According to the Pew Research Center, theists, agnostics, Jews, and Mormons score higher in religious knowledge than Protestants, outperforming them on questions about the core teachings and history of Christianity. Almost 60 percent of our youth leave their churches as young adults, with many of them joining the growing numbers of the so-called nones: those who profess no adherence to any faith whatsoever.[1]

Despite this unsettling news, the core message of Christianity, the gospel, is still capable of renewing the church. Rather than worrying or acting out of fear and self-preservation, we believe that the best hope for Christians, the Church, and the people who feel the pressures to abandon the faith, is the historic Christian faith, the gospel announcement of what God has done through Jesus Christ for the world.

SECOND, WE DESIGNED THIS STUDY TO SPEAK TO HONEST QUESTIONS.

Many in our Evangelical, Baptist, Reformed, Lutheran, and Anglican Churches have honest questions about faith and life that they may even be afraid to ask. Thus, we have sought to shape the material in this study to be of use to the concerns of long-time, committed Christians, new Christians, Christians with wavering faith, and skeptics alike.

We want this study to challenge skeptics and the growing numbers of people leaving the church, providing them with answers of substance and beauty, answers that give hope to the hopeless. We want this study to build the faith of Christians who have doubts. We want this study to give new Christians a firm grasp of the Christian faith. And we want to renew the faith of long-time committed Christians and equip them to better share the faith with others.

THIRD, WE DESIGNED THIS STUDY TO ENGAGE THE DRAMA OF SCRIPTURE, TEACH THE DOCTRINE OF HISTORIC CHRISTIANITY, MOVE TO DOXOLOGY, AND ENABLE HEALTHY DISCIPLESHIP.

It was really important to us that we handled doctrine in a way that shows how it naturally arises out of the Bible's narrative of Jesus Christ and his saving work.

FOURTH, WE DESIGNED THIS STUDY WITH AN EYE TOWARD SIMPLICITY AND A VARIETY OF SETTINGS.

We have thought of Sunday school classes, Bible study groups, informal gatherings among friends, and even individuals who want to learn more about the Christian faith. Thus, this study is arranged in a series of short sections, each of which could be done within an hour, with questions for personal reflection. The Leader's Edition of this study has group discussion questions so that Christians can come together to share insights, ask questions, pray for their churches and cities, and find hope to share what they are learning with friends and family.

In each lesson, there is a section to read followed by a set of questions for reflection. Questions for reflection are personal and not something you should feel obligated to share if meeting with a group. The Leader's Edition of this study includes questions for discussion at the end of every lesson. Questions for discussion are best discussed in a group where everyone can share their thoughts and questions.

---

[1] http://www.pewforum.org/2010/09/28/u-s-religious-knowledge-survey/

The best way to do this study is to work through one lesson a week. You can either read through all the sections and answer the reflection questions in one day or split up the sections and read one a day and answer the reflection questions until you finish the lesson. If meeting with a group, plan to meet once a week having read the lesson and answered the questions on your own first.

We have designed the questions for reflection and discussion with a practical emphasis to force you to engage the material in a prayerful way that should inspire worship and lead to a fuller understanding of how to live as a disciple of Christ. After each question, space has been provided for you to answer, but some people prefer to write their answers in a journal or notebook, and that is fine too!

HE WHO SAW IT HAS BORNE WITNESS—

HIS TESTIMONY IS TRUE, AND HE KNOWS

THAT HE IS TELLING THE TRUTH—

THAT YOU ALSO MAY BELIEVE.

—

JOHN 19:35

HISTORY,

Not

MYTHOLOGY

JOHN 19:35; 20:30-31; 21:24

READ

WHAT MAKES JOHN UNIQUE

The book of John is one of the most unique and beautiful books of the New Testament. John is very different from the other three Gospels in his storytelling, his style, and even his perspective. So much so that scholars call the other three the "Synoptic Gospels," coming from a Greek word that means "able to be seen together." They have many of the same stories in the same order, sometimes even using the same wording, while John's Gospel is in a world all its own. Over 90% of John's Gospel is original material not found in the other three.

In John, there is no Messianic secret, no driving out of demons, no parables. Many of the stories that are in all of the other three are missing from John. Rather than short pithy statements, the teaching comes in long discourses. John shares seven miracles of Jesus and seven "I Am" statements about Jesus. John uses lots of poetic language, metaphor, and symbolism to emphasize his theological points, weaving theology and history together.

Perhaps most distinctly, rather than placing the emphasis on the kingdom of God, John puts his emphasis on the person of Jesus. Beginning with a theological discussion of the Incarnation, John testifies that though Jesus was 100% divine, He was also a real person, in the flesh, who actually lived in human history. He came not only as the Messiah of the Jews, but the Savior of the world. In the Synoptics, salvation is primarily described as entrance into the kingdom, but in John it is described as knowing God and eternal life with Him through Jesus.

When John was writing this book, about 60 years after Christ's death and resurrection, false prophets were denying the Incarnation and the saving significance of Christ's death and resurrection. People were already starting to say it never happened. So the Gospel of John was written as a persuasive essay, to encourage believers that what they trusted in was true. John was not just writing a story; he was making a case, like a skilled lawyer in a courtroom. And we are the jury. We decide. Did John present enough evidence? Do we believe his story?

WHY JOHN WROTE HIS GOSPEL

In our introduction to John, we are actually starting at the end of the book. Because the end is where John explicitly stated why has written this book and what he wants us to do with it. It's the closing argument of his court case, the conclusion of his persuasive paper. When you write an academic persuasive paper, the basic structure is:

- → an introduction, where you state your hypothesis
- → the body, where you prove your hypothesis
- → the conclusion, where you restate your hypothesis, now that you have proven it

The three passages we will read today are that conclusion. John is declaring that he has proven his hypothesis. It's not just a statement of conclusion, then; it is a statement of confidence. He knows this to be true. He just spent a whole book proving it.

READ JOHN 19:35 AND 21:24

John assures us twice, at the ends of chapters 19 and 21, that he is an eyewitness to these events and that his testimony is true. He has shown us this throughout the book in the way it was written, sharing details and perspectives only an eyewitness could have known. But now he states it definitively. "I am an eyewitness to these things and my testimony is true." The stories about Jesus aren't fables or fairy tales. They are really true. They actually happened. They are history, not mythology.

Why does that matter? Why can't we just read the stories and glean the moral teaching out of it and let that be that? Why must the stories be true? Why can't we just say, "I think Jesus was a great moral teacher, but I don't know about this rising from the dead thing"?

Because if the resurrection didn't actually happen, then our faith is meaningless. In the book and subsequent film The Case for Christ, journalist Lee Strobel set out to disprove his wife's new faith in Christianity with what he saw as his greatest weapon—facts. One of his coworkers at the newspaper, a Christian with whom Lee had a contentious relationship, suggested if he really wanted to debunk Christianity, he should "go for the jugular" and focus on the question of Jesus's resurrection. He said, "The entire Christian faith hinges on the resurrection of Jesus. If it didn't happen, it's a house of cards."

Paul says the same thing in 1 Corinthians 15. If Christ was not raised, we have no hope in eternal life and "we are of all people most to be pitied" (v. 19). But also, we have no hope in this life. "Your faith is futile and you are still in your sins" (v. 17). The resurrection changes everything. If it didn't happen, our faith is nothing. If it did, our faith is everything. If Christ has not been raised, then nothing we do matters. This life doesn't matter. "If the dead are not raised, 'Let us eat and drink, for tomorrow we die'" (v. 32). But if He was raised, He defeated death for us. Which means both that we have hope in a future eternal life and that we have a purpose in this present life.

It is absolutely crucial to John that his readers know that the resurrection is fact. That it really happened. So, he makes these two very clear concluding statements. "This is true. I know it is true. I saw it with my own eyes." Then, sandwiched in the chapter in between these two statements, John shares his reason for writing it all down. We don't have to guess at his motivation, or what he wants us to know. Like a solid persuasive paper or closing argument to a court case, he tells us plainly.

QUESTIONS FOR REFLECTION

1. Do you have any friends who struggle with believing the stories in the Bible, particularly the miracles, the supernatural? If they asked you why you believed them, what would you say?

READ JOHN 20:30-31

So that we may believe and have eternal life. That's it. That's his whole purpose. Which is really the whole purpose of the Church too. Everything we do, everything we say, everything we donate money toward, everything we study, our whole mission. It is all so that the world may believe and have eternal life. That's it. This is the gospel, the good news of our faith. It's so simple and yet so pivotal. Much like the book of John itself.

Theologian Leon Morris wrote that many theologians have said that John's Gospel is like a pool in which a child may wade or an elephant can swim[2]. It is both simple and profound. On one level, a child can understand such simple concepts as the Light of the World or the Living Water. Yet even the most mature disciple can dig deep and mine riches from John's words. If you are a seeker or a new Christian, John is a great place to start to get to know Jesus. If you've been a Christian for decades, there are deep pools for you to dive into. So, as we read the book of John, as we study these ten theological truths that can be found here, dig deep. Ask the Holy Spirit to enlighten your reading of His Word.

---

[2] Leon Morris, *The Gospel According to John* (Grand Rapids: Eerdmans, 1971).

QUESTIONS FOR REFLECTION

1. What appeals to you about Jesus? Why were you drawn to Him?

2. What questions do you still have about Him? About the Christian faith or life?

3. What expectations or hopes do you have for this study? Why did you decide to join this study?

THE GOSPEL IN JOHN

These verses are the culmination, the conclusion, the "this is what the story has all been about." But this same gospel message was actually written over and over again throughout the whole story—the body of the persuasive paper. Most of us, when we think about the Gospel, just think of that classic verse, John 3:16. But John proves his hypothesis over and over in every chapter of the book.

→ "The water I give them will become in them a spring of water welling up to eternal life." John 4:14
→ "Whoever hears my word and believes Him who sent Me has eternal life." John 5:24
→ "Everyone who looks to the Son and believes in him shall have eternal life." John 6:40

And on and on and on. Eternal life, eternal life, eternal life. These are just three examples, but John proclaims the gospel at least forty times in his book, in slightly different ways (see Appendix A for a list of forty proclamations of the Gospel in John). When we look at these verses all together, it is next to impossible not to see that this is what this book is all about. Really, what all of the Gospels are about.

These four books aren't just called "The Stories of Jesus's Life." They're called the Gospels because through every story, through every teaching, through every miracle, they proclaim the gospel message. You cannot read the book of John without seeing it, crystal clear. This is why this book was written. This is what John wants us to believe.

Too many people read the Gospels, and really the whole Bible, primarily as a how-to book of morality. They focus on Jesus as a teacher and example of how to live. How to pray like Jesus, love like Jesus, forgive like Jesus, obey like Jesus. But John shows us that the purpose of the Bible is to point to Jesus as our Savior, not just our example. John doesn't portray Jesus as a moral teacher, but as the Resurrection and the Life.

We don't need a list of rules to follow. We need new hearts. We don't need behavior modification. We need to be made new creations (2 Corinthians 5:17). All the behavior modification in the world will never change our hearts. But God can change us from the inside out. We can follow Jesus's moral teachings only after we have been made new. Only through the power of the Holy Spirit working in us. Without Christ, we are dead in our trespasses and sins (Ephesians 2:1). Dead people can't follow moral laws. They need to be made alive.

This is the message of the book of John. If we believe in Jesus, we will have eternal life. Without Jesus, we are dead in our sins. With Jesus, we have life. Do we really believe that? Do we live like we really believe it? Do we tell others about it like we really believe it? As we study the book of John, let's read it with the gospel in mind. That we might ourselves be more confident in our belief, that we might live in a way that reflects it, and that we might persuade others to believe as well. It is truly a matter of life and death. Eternally.

APPENDIX A

FORTY PROCLAMATIONS OF THE GOSPEL IN JOHN

"Look, the Lamb of God, who takes away the sin of the world! . . . The man on whom you see the Spirit come down and remain is the one who will baptize with the Holy Spirit. . . . I have seen and I testify that this is God's Chosen One." 1:29-34

Nathanael declared, "Rabbi, you are the Son of God. You are the King of Israel." *1:49*

"No one can see the Kingdom of God unless they are born again." *3:3*

"The Son of Man must be lifted up, that everyone who believes may have eternal life in Him." *3:15*

"For God so loved the world that He gave His one and only Son, that whoever believes in Him shall not perish, but have eternal life." *3:16*

"Whoever believes in the Son has eternal life, but whoever rejects the Son will not see life, for God's wrath remains on them." *3:36*

"Whoever drinks the water I give them will never thirst. Indeed, the water I give them will become in them a spring of water welling up to eternal life." *4:14*

"I, the one speaking to you–I am [the Messiah]." *4.25*

"We know that this man really is the Savior of the world." *4:42*

"Whoever hears my word and believes Him who sent Me has eternal life and will not be judged but has crossed over from death to life." *5:24*

"You study the Scriptures diligently because you think that in them you have eternal life. These are the very Scriptures that testify about Me, yet you refuse to come to Me to have life." *5:39-40*

"Do not work for food that spoils, but for food that endures to eternal life, which the Son of Man will give you. For on Him, God the Father has placed His seal of approval." *6:27*

"The work of God is this: to believe in the One He has sent." *6:29*

Then Jesus declared, "I am the bread of life. Whoever comes to me will never go hungry, and whoever believes in me will never be thirsty." *6:35*

"For my Father's will is that everyone who looks to the Son and believes in him shall have eternal life, and I will raise them up at the last day." *6:40*

"I am the living bread that came down from heaven. Whoever eats this bread will live forever. This bread is my flesh, which I will give for the life of the world." *6:51*

"Whoever eats my flesh and drinks my blood has eternal life, and I will raise them up at the last day." *6:54*

Simon Peter answered him, "Lord, to whom shall we go? You have the words of eternal life. We have come to believe and to know that you are the Holy One of God." *6:68-69*

On the last and greatest day of the festival, Jesus stood and said in a loud voice, "Let anyone who is thirsty come to me and drink. Whoever believes in me, as Scripture has said, rivers of living water will flow from within them." *7:37*

When Jesus spoke again to the people, he said, "I am the light of the world. Whoever follows me will never walk in darkness, but will have the light of life." *8:12*

To the Jews who had believed him, Jesus said, "If you hold to my teaching, you are really my disciples. Then you will know the truth, and the truth will set you free." *8:31-32*

"Very truly I tell you, whoever obeys my word will never see death." *8:51*

"Very truly I tell you," Jesus answered, "before Abraham was born, I am!" *8:58*

"While I am in the world, I am the light of the world." *9:5*

Jesus heard that they had thrown him out, and when he found him, he said, "Do you believe in the Son of Man?" "Who is he, sir?" the man asked. "Tell me so that I may believe in him." Jesus said, "You have now seen him; in fact, he is the one speaking with you." Then the man said, "Lord, I believe," and he worshiped him. *9:35-38*

"I am the gate; whoever enters through me will be saved." *10:9*

"I have come that they may have life, and have it to the full." *10:9-10*

"I lay down my life for the sheep." *10:15*

"My sheep listen to my voice; I know them, and they follow me. I give them eternal life, and they shall never perish; no one will snatch them out of my hand." *10:27-28*

Jesus said to her, "I am the resurrection and the life. The one who believes in me will live, even though they die; and whoever lives by believing in me will never die. Do you believe this?" *11:25-26*

"I, when I am lifted up from the earth, will draw all people to myself." He said this to show the kind of death he was going to die. *12:32-33*

"I have come into the world as a light, so that no one who believes in me should stay in darkness." 12:46

"I did not come to judge the world, but to save the world." *12:47*

"[The Father's] command leads to eternal life. So whatever I say is just what the Father has told me to say." *12:50*

"Whoever accepts me accepts the one who sent me." *13:20*

"And if I go and prepare a place for you, I will come back and take you to be with me that you also may be where I am." *14:3*

Jesus answered, "I am the way and the truth and the life. No one comes to the Father except through me." *14:6*

"You heard me say, 'I am going away and I am coming back to you.' If you loved me, you would be glad that I am going to the Father, for the Father is greater than I. I have told you now before it happens, so that when it does happen you will believe." *14:28-29*

"Now this is eternal life: that they know you, the only true God, and Jesus Christ, whom you have sent." *17:3*

Jesus told him, "Because you have seen me, you have believed; blessed are those who have not seen and yet have believed." *20:29*

AND THE WORD BECAME FLESH

AND DWELT AMONG US, AND WE

HAVE SEEN HIS GLORY, GLORY AS OF

THE ONLY SON FROM THE FATHER, FULL

OF GRACE AND TRUTH.

—

JOHN 1:14

The WORD MADE FLESH

JOHN 1:1–18

READ

POETIC FORM OF THE PASSAGE

In the original language, this introduction to the Gospel of John has every appearance of being a poem with prose commentary interspersed throughout:

- → vv. 1–5: poetry (five couplets)
- → vv. 6–9: prose commentary
- → vv. 10–11: poetry (two couplets)
- → vv. 12–13: prose commentary
- → vv. 14: poetry (three couplets)
- → vv. 15–16: prose commentary
- → v. 17: poetry (one couplet)
- → v. 18: prose commentary

This poetic opening feels like a hymn in praise of something so awe-inspiring and incredible that it almost can't be put into words. The Incarnation. God become man. Word made flesh. This mystery of mysteries. John uses this lofty language to inspire awe and worship of Christ from the very beginning of his Gospel. In John's view, Jesus is not just a moral teacher or a wise prophet. He is God Himself.

READ JOHN 1:1–13

John opens his Gospel with "In the beginning," the very same words used in Genesis 1:1, intentionally connecting the Incarnation to Creation. John doesn't start with the birth of Jesus or His genealogy or the first acts of His ministry. He goes all the way back to Creation. For a very specific reason. To tell us from the very beginning of the Gospel that Jesus Christ is God Himself. John's opening gets right to the point. We don't have to wait to find out who Jesus is.

JESUS IS THE WORD

Logos, translated as "the Word," is capitalized here in the English text (following the Greek manuscripts), clearly personifying the Word. In the Old Testament, the "Word" was understood theologically as personified divine wisdom (Job 28:12; Proverbs 8, 9). Jewish doctrine taught that wisdom existed before the rest of creation and that God created all things through wisdom, but that wisdom itself was created by God. So John borrowed a term from Jewish doctrine, but he went beyond the Jewish understanding. He declared that the Word actually existed from before the beginning, with God, and even *was* God.

By calling Jesus "the Word," John called Him the embodiment of all of God's revelation in Scripture. Everything God says in Scripture we see in Jesus. Jesus not only teaches us God's Word, but He is also God's Word in the flesh. Jesus is the manifestation of God's wisdom. Jesus is "the light of men, the light that shines in the darkness" (John 1:4–5). "The true light, which gives light to everyone" (John 1:9). The light that illuminates our understanding. Some have said Jesus is the Word because He is "everything God wanted to say to the world." Jesus Himself said God's written word bears witness to Him (John 5:39) and He is the fulfillment of all of the Scriptures (Matthew 5:17). Though we can and should share God's written word, the Bible, with people, the simplest way to introduce them to God's Word is to simply show them Jesus. This is John's focus through his whole Gospel. Point to Jesus. Show them Jesus.

QUESTIONS FOR REFLECTION

1. How can we show Jesus to the people in our lives?

2. Do you know where to go in the Bible to point people to Jesus?

3. What is the most important thing you think people need to know about Jesus? Where would you find that explained or illustrated in the Bible?

THE WORD WAS WITH GOD AND THE WORD WAS GOD

John describes the Trinity and the Incarnation using terms that would have been familiar to the Jews of the day, but he redefines those terms, completely changing their understanding. If we look back to Genesis 1, we see two persons of the Trinity clearly—God the Father and the Holy Spirit. "The Spirit of God was hovering over the face of the waters" (Genesis 1:2). But John is telling us that Jesus was also there by using this name, "the Word," for Him. In the Greek version of Genesis 1, we see the verb form of *logos* when God spoke creation into being. "And God said . . ." God spoke creation into being through His Word. Therefore, "all things were made through him" (John 1:3).

Over the centuries, many people have tried to use metaphors or similes to explain the Trinity, but no metaphor can completely capture what the Trinity is, only *some* of what it is like. All explanations we have ever attempted have fallen short and eventually have led to heresy. What we do know about the Trinity is:

→   God exists in three distinct persons. It is not one person who changes forms for different situations or times. We see all three in one place at one time at Jesus's baptism (Matthew 3:13–17).

→   Each person is fully God. Neither Jesus nor the Holy Spirit were created by God. This point was argued at the Council of Nicea in AD 325, where they used the phrase "begotten, not made" to describe Jesus (Philippians 2:6–7).

→   There is only one God, not three different gods. Though God exists in three distinct persons, those persons are completely unified, with no separation, as one being (Mark 12:29).

They are all one and all equal. And yet, when He became man, Jesus humbled Himself. "He did not count equality with God a thing to be grasped" (Philippians 2:6). He made Himself nothing, "taking the form of a servant. . . . He humbled Himself by becoming obedient to the point of death, even death on a cross" (Philippians 2:7–8). He willingly submitted Himself to the Father (Mark 14:36). He was sent by the Father into the world (John 20:21), yet He and the Father remained one (John 10:30). The Trinity is something we may not completely understand with our finite minds. It is a holy mystery, but one we must confess to be true. As John describes with such elegance, the gospel requires one God in three persons—Father, Son, and Holy Spirit. It is a holy mystery.

THE PRE-INCARNATE CHRIST

Scholars use the term "the pre-incarnate Christ" to describe appearances of Christ in the Bible before the Incarnation. Before He actually put on flesh and became the man, Jesus of Nazareth, He existed from before the beginning with God the Father and the Holy Spirit. In the Old Testament, we see Him temporarily appear in human form many times in what theologians call a "Christophany" (literally, "appearance of Christ"). In those appearances, He is called "the angel of the Lord," which didn't actually mean He was an angel. The word *angel* means "messenger," so the term described His role as "the messenger of the Lord."

We know these appearances are not just any messenger, not just an angel, because the people to whom He appears treat Him as God himself. For example, in Genesis 16:7–14, it is "the angel of the Lord" who appears to Hagar and speaks to her. But verse 13 says, "She called the name of the Lord who spoke to her, 'You are a God of seeing.'" In the story of the burning bush in Exodus 3, it was "the angel of the Lord" in verse 2 and "the Lord" in verse 4. And in verse 6, He said He was God. "I am the God of your father, the God of Abraham, the God of Isaac, and the God of Jacob." When He appeared to Joshua, He said what he had said to Moses at the burning bush, "Take off your sandals from your feet, for the place where you are standing is holy" (Joshua 5:15). In the call of Gideon in Judges 6, He was "the angel of the Lord" in verse 11 and "the Lord" in verses 14 and 16. When Samson's father Manoah realized who He was, Manoah said, "We shall surely die, for we have seen God" (Judges 13:22). There is a similar interplay in all of these appearances, making it clear that this "messenger of the Lord" was not just an angel. He was God Himself in human form.

This pre-incarnate Christ appeared to Abraham outside his tent (Genesis 18:1–3) and wrestled with Jacob until daybreak (Genesis 32:22–32). He appeared to Joshua before the battle of Jericho to encourage him that God was with him (Joshua 5:13–15). He appeared to Samson's mother to tell her she would bear a son (Judges 13:3–24) and to Gideon to call him to battle (Judges 6:11–21). Though we do not see the Son take on a permanent human body until the Incarnation, the pre-incarnate Christ wasn't sitting up in heaven twiddling his thumbs until it was His time to come. The Son and the Spirit and the Father were all active in human history from the beginning.

"I AM"

At the very beginning of his Gospel, John makes the audacious claim that Jesus *is* God. And he shows us again and again. Jesus called God His own Father, "making himself equal with God" (John 5:18), an intimacy the Jews at that time did not claim. Jesus said, "I and the Father are one" (John 10:30). Thomas called Jesus "my Lord and my God!" (John 20:28). And with every "I Am" statement Jesus makes, He reiterates that He is God.

The name "Yahweh," God's personal name in the Old Testament, means "I Am." It comes from God's appearing to Moses at the burning bush. Until this point in biblical history, God had only revealed Himself as El Shaddai, God Almighty. But here, when Moses asks Him who he should say sent him to rescue them, God gives Moses His personal name, "I Am Who I Am . . . Say this to the people of Israel, 'I Am has sent me to you'" (Exodus 3:14). In the next verse He says, "This is my name forever" (v. 15).

God's name is I Am because He has always existed and always will exist. He is the source of all that is. He is the only God; there is no other (Isaiah 45:5). There is no one like Him (Jeremiah 10:6). We cannot change Him. We cannot control Him. We cannot make Him out to be who we want Him to be. He is who He is.

In the book of John, Jesus intentionally uses seven "I Am" statements, not only to tell us what He is like but to show that He is the great I Am, Yahweh himself. When the people challenged Jesus about something He said about Abraham, He answered them, "Before Abraham was, I Am" (John 8:58). The crowds saw this as Jesus claiming to be God, and they immediately tried to stone Him for blasphemy (v. 59). Each one of the "I Am" statements connects Jesus to God the Father:

"I am the bread of life" (John 6:35, 48, 51)—"Man shall not live by bread alone, but man lives by every word that comes from the mouth of the Lord" (Deuteronomy 8:3).

→ "I am the light of the world" (8:12; 9:5)—"Your word is a lamp to my feet and a light to my path" (Psalm 119:105).

→ "I am the door of the sheep" (10:7, 9)—"The Lord is my shepherd. . . . He leads me in paths of righteousness for his name's sake" (Psalm 23:1, 3).

→ "I am the good shepherd" (10:11, 14)—"He will tend his flock like a shepherd" (Isaiah 40:11; see also Psalm 23; Jeremiah 50:6; Ezekiel 34:11–24; Micah 5:4).

→ "I am the resurrection and the life" (11:25)—"See now that I, even I, am he, and there is no god beside me; I kill and I make alive . . . and there is none that can deliver out of my hand" (Deuteronomy 32:39).

→ "I am the way, the truth, and the life" (14:6)—"Prepare the way of the Lord" (Isaiah 40:3).

→ "I am the true vine" (15:1)—"Your mother [Israel] was like a vine in your vineyard, planted by the water, fruitful and full of branches" (Ezekiel 19:10).

Jesus says He gives "living water" (John 4:10–11; 7:37–39) just as God is the "fountain of living water" (Jeremiah 2:13; 17:13). When He describes Himself as the Good Shepherd, He uses language almost identical to that which God used of Himself in Deuteronomy. "I, even I, am he, and there is no god beside me. I kill and I make alive. I would and I heal, and there is none that can deliver out of my hand" (Deuteronomy 32:39). Jesus said, "I give them eternal life, and they will never perish. No one will snatch them out of my hand. My Father, who has given them to me, is greater than all, and no one is able to snatch them out of the Father's hand" (John 10:28–29). And then He punctuates that reference by saying, "I and the Father are one" (John 10:30). And once again, the people picked up stones to kill Him for blasphemy because, with that statement, He was claiming to be God (John 10:33).

Jesus replied, "Do you say of him whom the Father consecrated and sent into the world, 'You are blaspheming,' because I said, 'I am the Son of God'? If I am not doing the works of my Father, then do not believe me; but if I do them, even though you do not believe me, believe the works, that you may know and understand that the Father is in me and I am in the Father" (John 10:36–38). John leaves no room for doubt about who Jesus claimed to be or who John believed Him to be. Jesus is God.

QUESTIONS FOR REFLECTION

1. Why does it matter that Jesus *is* God? How does that affect the meaning of His death and resurrection?

2. Why is Jesus worthy of our worship?

3. If a friend said to you, "The God of the Old Testament seems so mean and Jesus seems so loving. How can they be the same God?" what would you say?

READ JOHN 1:14–18

THE WORD BECAME FLESH AND DWELLED AMONG US

Neither Greek philosophers nor Jewish teachers could conceive of the Word becoming flesh. Since the time of Plato, Greek philosophers had emphasized that the ideal was what was invisible and eternal rather than physical and temporary. Most Jews emphasized the vast distinction between the Creator and His creation, so they never even imagined God becoming human. This thought would have been shocking to them. Christ came in the flesh to redeem our flesh. John wanted to be sure his readers knew that Jesus really did come to earth in human form. He lived, ate, slept, sweated, and cried. He really was God with skin on.

The word we translate as "dwelt" in John 1:14 is *skénoó,* which means "to encamp, to pitch one's tent." This is certainly a reference to the tabernacle in the Old Testament, where the Spirit of the Lord dwelled with His people. Just as the Lord pitched His tent among the Israelites, in the center of their camp, Jesus pitched His tent among His people and lived and walked and talked among them. Only this time, it wasn't a tent containing an ark and other holy objects, but a man in the flesh. A person you could see and hear and touch.

Before the tabernacle was built, Moses used to pitch a tent far outside the camp, which he called "the tent of meeting." Anyone who sought the Lord would go out to the tent, where Moses would speak with God on their behalf. When Moses entered the tent, the pillar of cloud—the Spirit of God—would descend to the entrance of the tent and the Lord would speak with Moses "face to face, as a man speaks to his friend" (Exodus 33:7–11). Because Moses's face shone after he spoke with God, the people were afraid to come near him. So, Moses would wear a veil over his face to speak to the people but take it off when he spoke with God (Exodus 34:29–35). Because they could not be in God's presence, they could not behold his glory.

But when they built the tabernacle, God told them to put it directly in the middle of their camp, not outside the camp like the tent of meeting had been. Over and over in the old covenant, God promised to dwell with them, to walk with them, to be their God, to be in relationship with them (e.g., Exodus 6:7; 29:45; Leviticus 26:12; Jeremiah 7:23; 11:4; 30:22; Ezekiel 36:28). He wasn't some distant God up in the cosmos who took no active role in the day-to-day life of His people. The word we translate from the Hebrew as "tabernacle" means "dwelling place" or "tent." God literally pitched His tent in the center of their camp. The God of the universe, Creator of all things, lived in a tent among His people, right down there in the middle of their mess.

This is exactly what Jesus did in the Incarnation, but in a new and more permanent way. Instead of being invisible in the tabernacle/temple, Jesus came in the flesh and dwelled among us. The name Immanuel means "God with us" (Isaiah 7:14; Matthew 1:23). During His time on earth, Jesus was the dwelling place of God on earth. He was God's temple (John 2:20–21), no longer a building but a person. Jesus literally dwelled among His people. Just as God dwelled in a tent in close quarters with the twelve tribes, Jesus lived in close quarters with His twelve disciples every day. Just as God walked with His people, Jesus walked with the disciples.

But Jesus was able to go even further. Because God's Spirit dwelled in Him as a person instead of in a building, people didn't have to go to a place to meet with God. God in the form of Jesus came to them. Because He was God in human form, He was able to go into places and meet with people who would never have set foot in the temple. Tax collectors, prostitutes, lepers—the unclean who wouldn't have been allowed in the temple even if they had wanted to go. In the Incarnation, Jesus came down to us, in the middle of our mess. In *The Message,* Eugene Peterson translates John 1:14, "The Word became flesh and blood, and moved into the neighborhood."

Later, through His death and resurrection, we were given even fuller access to the Spirit. The veil of the temple, which separated God's Spirit from the people, was torn in two (Matthew 27:51). The Holy Spirit was poured out on all the people (Acts 2). Instead of just being near Jesus, the disciples were given the Holy Spirit *inside* them. They became temples of God themselves (2 Corinthians 6:16). In the old covenant, God's Spirit was external—in a building, in a cloud, on a mountain, in a bush, coming upon people. Because God's Spirit dwelled in Jesus, a man, in the Incarnation, his death and resurrection made it possible for the Spirit to become internal, to dwell in the hearts of his people. That is what made the new covenant new.

Through Christ, those of us who have accepted Jesus are able to look upon the glory of God "with unveiled face" (2 Corinthians 3:18). Because of Christ, we can stand before the throne of God with confidence (Hebrews 4:16; 13:10). Because of Christ, we have full access to God all the time. In the new covenant, we have the Spirit not just beside us or before us in battle. Not just in a building where we can go ask him for His help. We have Him inside us. He abides in us. He remains in us. This is not a temporary thing. The Spirit does not come and go from us. He stays and he dwells in us. He pitches his tent in our hearts.

In the Incarnation, Jesus came to where we lived and made his home here with us. Jesus didn't stay in heaven with God, enjoying being holy together, and leaving us in our mess. He came into our unholy mess, to the fishermen and the prostitutes, the lepers and the tax collectors. He met people where they were and brought God's Spirit to *them*. He created a home for us where we can live and dwell with God—not separated by a veil in a temple but in a face-to-face relationship. This is what makes Christianity different from every other religion. In other religions, we have to do x, y, and z to get to God. In Christianity, God knew that no matter what we did we could never get to him, so he came to us.

THE NEXT DAY HE SAW JESUS

COMING TOWARD HIM, AND SAID,

"BEHOLD, THE LAMB OF GOD, WHO

TAKES AWAY THE SIN OF THE WORLD!

THIS IS HE OF WHOM I SAID,

'AFTER ME COMES A MAN WHO

RANKS BEFORE ME, BECAUSE

HE WAS BEFORE ME.'"

—

JOHN 1:29-30

The LAMB
of GOD

JOHN 1:29-51

READ JOHN 1:29-37

After the deeply theological introduction about the divinity and humanity of Christ, John starts with the testimony of John the Baptist. It is the first thing he wants us to know—who John the Baptist said Jesus was. In this short passage, John the Baptist calls Jesus both "the Lamb of God" and "the Son of God."

John the Baptist was a cousin of Jesus, who was born only a few months before him and also had a supernatural conception. John's mother had been barren, but the Lord opened her womb and told his father that John would be a prophet like Elijah who would "turn the hearts of the fathers to the children and the disobedient to the wisdom of the just, to make ready for the Lord a people prepared" (Luke 1:17). John the Baptist was the prophet who would prepare the way for Jesus. He is a key figure in all of the Gospels, but only in the Gospel of John does he call Jesus "the Lamb of God" (John 1:29, 36). In fact, this title is used only twice in Scripture, in these two verses. But that doesn't mean it was a title that John the Baptist invented. It came from his deep knowledge of the Old Testament.

OLD TESTAMENT BACKGROUND

Although the exact phrase "Lamb of God" never appears in the Old Testament, there are several allusions to it—all of which point ahead to Christ and His sacrifice on the cross. It is a theological concept that runs all the way through redemptive history.

THE (ALMOST) SACRIFICE OF ISAAC (GENESIS 22)

In this story, God does what from our vantage point seems unthinkable. He asks Abraham to offer his son, his "only son"—not the only son he had, but the only son of Abraham and Sarah. Isaac was the son God had given him, the son of promise, the one through whom all the promises to Abraham would be fulfilled. And Abraham obeyed. As crazy as it sounds to us, it probably sounded even crazier to him. What was God doing? Why would He have Abraham and Sarah go through all they had gone through just to take Isaac away?

But Abraham obeyed. He trusted God. God had shown Abraham in the past what happened when he tried to do things his own way. God had shown Himself to be faithful, and Abraham knew God would keep His promises. If God really was going to have him offer Isaac, then He would provide another way—perhaps even raise Isaac from the dead (Hebrews 11:19).

At that time, other religions in the region practiced child sacrifice, because their gods demanded it. But our God completely forbids child sacrifice in His law. Not just sacrifice to false gods, but any child sacrifice at all (Leviticus 18:21; Deuteronomy 12:31). This story is not about child sacrifice, but about God's subversion of it. Instead of God asking us to sacrifice our children to Him, He would sacrifice His son for us.

Theologians call this a substitutionary sacrifice. If we look closely at the structure of the story and how it unfolds, we can see this theological point being made by what Abraham says to Isaac at the beginning of the story (v. 8) and in what he names the mountain at the end of it (v. 14): "God will provide for himself the lamb for the burnt offering, my son" (v. 8) and "The Lord will provide" (v. 14). In this story, God literally provides an animal as a substitution for the sacrifice of Abraham's son, but it was a model for a much greater substitution. One day, God Himself would become the lamb. He would offer His Son, His only Son, to die in our place.

THE PASSOVER LAMB (EXODUS 12)

We can see Jesus as the Lamb of God even more clearly in the Passover. When God sent the final plague over the Egyptians, the death of the firstborn son of each household, He instructed His people to slay unblemished lambs and spread the blood on their doorposts. The angel of death would pass over any house that was covered with the blood of the lamb (Exodus 12:3–13).

Jesus is the new Passover lamb. He even died on the day of the Preparation of the Passover (John 19:14). But the blood of Jesus did more than stop the angel of death one time. His sacrifice conquered death forever (2 Timothy 1:10; Hebrews 2:14). Everyone who is covered by the blood of this Passover lamb will not die but have eternal life (John 3:16; 11:25).

THE SACRIFICIAL SYSTEM (LEVITICUS 1-7; 16)

After the Passover, God rescued His people from Egypt and brought them to the land He had promised Abraham so they He could be their God and they could be His people. At Mount Sinai, He gave them the Law, which set up the way they were to live under the leadership of God, their King. This Law included a system for offering sacrifices. Five kinds of offerings are discussed in Leviticus 1–7, three of which are relationship offerings and two of which are offered for atonement for sin.

In every offering, something significant was done with the blood of the animal, because "the life of the animal is in the blood" (Leviticus 17:14). In the relationship offerings, the blood was either sprinkled around the altar or thrown on the side of the altar. In the two atonement offerings, the blood was even more significant. The Hebrew word *atone* means "to cover." In these offerings, the blood of the animal covered the sin and washed it clean. The reparation (guilt) offering was given to make restitution for sin. They had to pay back whatever they had damaged plus one-fifth and offer a sacrifice. In the reparation offering, the blood was "scattered abundantly" around the altar. The purification (or sin) offering was used to purify the tabernacle/temple from the sin that had been brought upon it by the people. The temple was God's dwelling place and God cannot dwell with sin. In a typical purification offering, the blood of the lamb was actually smeared on the four corners of the altar and sprinkled on the curtain to the Holy of Holies, which would make the people holy once again.

But once a year, on The Day of Atonement, the high priest would offer a purification offering for the whole nation for the whole year. He went into the Holy of Holies and put the blood on the mercy seat of the Ark of the Covenant. All the other times, he only sprinkled the altar and the veil. But once a year, he actually sprinkled the blood on the ark itself, the dwelling place of the Holy Spirit (Leviticus 16).

In the old covenant, the priests had to offer these sacrifices day after day, year after year. But when Jesus came, His sacrifice was once and for all. His blood washes us clean forever (1 John 1:7). Jesus was both the High Priest and the sacrificial Lamb of a better covenant. The writer of Hebrews explains to us that the tabernacle in the old covenant was a mere "copy and shadow of the heavenly things" (Hebrews 8:5). But when Christ came, He didn't enter the copy, He entered heaven itself (Hebrews 9:24).

"He entered once for all into the holy places, not by means of the blood of goats and calves but by means of his own blood, thus securing an eternal redemption. For if the blood of goats and bulls, and the sprinkling of defiled persons with the ashes of a heifer, sanctify for the purification of the flesh, how much more will the blood of Christ, who through the eternal Spirit offered himself without blemish to God, purify our conscience from dead works to serve the living God" (Hebrews 9:12–14).

Jesus is our purification offering. His blood sanctifies, purifies, and cleanses us, we who are the temple of the new covenant (e.g., 1 Corinthians 6:11; Titus 2:14). He offered Himself as the reparation offering—to make reparation for our sins. His blood paid our debt. "You were ransomed from the futile ways inherited from your forefathers, not with perishable things such as silver or gold, but with the precious blood of Christ, like that of a lamb without blemish or spot" (1 Peter 1:18–19).

THE SUFFERING SERVANT (ISAIAH 53)

In the books of the prophets, many of the prophecies about the coming Messiah paint Him as a victorious warrior. But victory for Jesus looked very different from the victory we typically see in the world. The world conquers with brute force; Jesus conquered with self-sacrifice. He was a servant King, characterized by humility and gentleness. He didn't lead revolutions; He washed feet. He didn't gather an army; He healed the sick and preached selfless love. He didn't lead His disciples into a battle to conquer the Romans and sit on the throne of Israel. He walked alone into His battle on the cross, where He won the victory by dying.

Jesus's victory was not won with swords or chariots, because His battle was not against flesh and blood, but against death itself. Death could only be overcome by His resurrection. Victory could only come through sacrifice. The prophet Isaiah paints the picture of this Suffering Servant, who like a lamb led to the slaughter, was crushed for our iniquities and pierced for our transgressions. Jesus was made "an offering for guilt," which in Hebrew is the same word for reparation offering. His blood paid our debt. By His wounds, we are healed (Isaiah 53).

QUESTIONS FOR REFLECTION

1. What do all of these images say about how God views sin? Why is sin a big deal to God?

2. Many people believe that God saves those who try their best and are basically "good people." What does Christ's sacrifice say about that view?

3. Where in your life do you need to submit to God in obedience like Christ?

4. Read Romans 12:1–2. What does Paul tell believers about how to offer sacrifices in the new covenant?

READ JOHN 1:29–37 AGAIN, KNOWING NOW THE OLD TESTAMENT BACKGROUND OF THE TERM "LAMB OF GOD"

THE TESTIMONY OF JOHN THE BAPTIST

This is the first image John paints of who Jesus is—"Behold the Lamb of God who takes away the sins of the world." This is why He came. From the very beginning, John makes it clear that Jesus came to die for our sins. Whatever else He will teach, whatever miracles He will do, this is His mission. This is His purpose. The Son of God who became the Lamb of God.

→ This is the gospel. That God so loved the world that He sent His only son to die for us (John 3:16).
→ This is love. That God sent Jesus to die as an atoning sacrifice for our sins (1 John 4:10).

Jesus Himself said there is no greater expression of love than dying for those you love (John 15:13). For John, this is love. This is who Jesus is, first and foremost: God made flesh who came to die for us—out of His great love.

When John the Baptist called out to the disciples, "Behold, the Lamb of God," it wasn't merely an observation. It was a directive to follow Jesus. He wasn't saying, "Oh hey, there's the Lamb of God!" He was telling them to go follow Him. Two of his disciples "heard him say this, and they followed Jesus" (John 1:37). His purpose in saying it was to get them to follow Jesus, which is what we see happening through the rest of the chapter.

John the Baptist had no problem saying he was not the One; that he was there only to point to Him. In fact, the Gospel writer says, "He confessed, and he did not deny, but confessed, 'I am not the Christ'" (v. 20). The NIV says, "He confessed freely." John the Baptist even went so far to say that he was not worthy to untie the strap of Jesus's sandal (v. 27). Later he says, "He must increase, but I must decrease" (John 3:30). This was not a man out for his own glory. Like a true servant of the Lord, John pointed his disciples to Jesus, because his entire purpose was to point to Jesus. He was just the messenger. His whole ministry was to prepare the way for Jesus (John 1:29–31).

We are also messengers, just like John the Baptist. We have been sent to point people to Jesus, to direct people to follow Him (Matthew 28:19–20; Acts 1:8). Yet sometimes, we are afraid to share the gospel. Afraid we won't know what to say or that we'll offend someone. Afraid we're not "good enough Christians" to be a witness or that people just don't want to hear it. We share good news with friends and family, however, every day. We rave about that great movie we just saw or the restaurant we just tried, or the amazing new trick we found on the Internet for getting stains out of that white dress shirt.

The gospel message is monumentally more important than any of those things we so freely share. The gospel is not just good news, it's the best news. It's life-changing news. It is life-saving news. Our joy and thankfulness for what God has done in Christ should overflow into our conversations and our day-to-day life. Like John the Baptist, our excitement about Jesus should lead us to point others to Him.

QUESTIONS FOR REFLECTION

1. What was John the Baptist saying about Jesus?

2. Put yourself in John the Baptist's place. What would it have felt like to see Jesus, the Messiah that Israel had been waiting centuries for?

3. Why would he send his own disciples to follow Jesus? What does this say about John the Baptist? What does it say about his view of Christ?

4. What causes us to fear sharing the gospel message with others? How can we overcome those fears?

5. How would you explain to someone the good news that Jesus is both the Son of God and the Lamb of God?

READ JOHN 1:38–50

THE FIRST DISCIPLES

Rabbi, Messiah, Jesus of Nazareth, Son of God, King of Israel, Son of Man. We get an onslaught of titles for Jesus in this very first chapter. John is giving us a multifaceted identification of Jesus from the beginning. But it is all framed by His identity as the Lamb of God, His ultimate purpose. He is a rabbi (teacher), but this is not His ultimate purpose. He is the Messiah who will be sacrificed as the Lamb of God, not the conquering hero they may have imagined. He is both Jesus of Nazareth and Son of God, both human and divine. He is the King of Israel, but not the king they were expecting. His kingdom is not of this world. He is the Son of Man, the One to whom God the Father gives an everlasting dominion, a kingdom that will never be destroyed (Daniel 7:13–14). All of these titles are built into the framework of the Lamb of God. The rabbi, the Messiah, the King, the Son of God, the Son of Man is a Suffering Servant. His victory will be accomplished through sacrifice.

These are the only stories in John of the calling of the disciples. John's account is very much the story of people pointing others to Jesus, one after another. First John the Baptist pointed Andrew and another unnamed disciple to Jesus, and Andrew brought Peter to Jesus (v. 35–42). Then Jesus called Philip, and Philip brought Nathanael to Jesus (v. 46). This wasn't a strategic evangelism plan. It was simply people pointing other people to Jesus. Relational evangelism. "We've found the Messiah. . . . Come and see" (v. 41, 45–46). They met Jesus and were so excited about Him that they went and found their friends and family and said, "You've got to come see this!" Because it was such good news, they had to share it.

Evangelism really doesn't have to be more than that. "I've found the way, the truth, and the life. . . . Come and see." We don't have to have a master's degree in apologetics. We don't have to know the answer to every theological question, or have a prepared speech, or have our lives perfectly put together. We just need to point people to Jesus. Because, just like John the Baptist, it's not about us; it's about Jesus. It has been said that the church isn't a museum for saints; it's a hospital for sinners (this phrase has been attributed to Abigail Van Buren, "Dear Abby," but it's uncertain whether she originated the phrase or not). In the same way, evangelism is simply one sick person telling another sick person where to find the doctor. We are not the doctor ourselves; we only point to Him (Mark 2:17).

QUESTIONS FOR REFLECTION

1. What other titles did the disciples use for Jesus in this passage? What title did Jesus use for Himself?

2. How did they all relate to the "Lamb of God"?

"NO ONE HAS ASCENDED

INTO HEAVEN EXCEPT HE

WHO DESCENDED FROM HEAVEN,

THE SON OF MAN."

—

JOHN 3:13

BORN *from* ABOVE

READ JOHN 3:1–13

BORN FROM ABOVE

In chapter 3, the text once again becomes deeply theological. John uses rich symbolism, like wind and water and birth and weddings. He uses stark contrasts between flesh and spirit, light and darkness, earthly and heavenly. He uses plays on words like *wind* and *spirit*.

In chapter 1, after Jesus called His first disciples, He performed His first miracle at a wedding in Cana (John 2:1–11) and then went to Jerusalem and cleansed the temple from those who had made it into a marketplace (John 2:13–25). In these first few chapters, we see the beginnings of Jesus's ministry as well as people's first reactions to Him. The Jewish leaders challenged His authority—asking why He felt He had the right to cleanse the temple (John 2:18). But many believed in His name because of the signs He was doing (John 2:23). Others probably fell somewhere between belief and doubt. One of them was a man named Nicodemus.

NICODEMUS

Nicodemus is a fascinating character. He was a Pharisee and "a member of the Jewish ruling council," the Sanhedrin. Theologically for John, this title connects Nicodemus with the elite Jewish leadership who opposed Jesus (John 7:45–50). He was a member of the ruling class, not a simple fisherman like many of Jesus's disciples. He was from the capital city of Jerusalem, not the "backwoods" of Galilee. Judeans tended to look down on Galileans, viewing them as uneducated, of questionable ancestry, and as rabble-rousers. Nicodemus was a pious man, not a "sinner" like many of the others who came to Jesus (Matthew 11:19). By giving us three glimpses of Nicodemus throughout his book, John shows us that even some of Jesus's greatest opponents can become His followers.

Although John doesn't tell us here how Nicodemus responds to Jesus, we do see him two more times in the book of John. At the end of chapter seven, after Jesus announced publicly at the Feast of Booths that He was the living water, Nicodemus sort of defended Jesus. He told the rest of the Pharisees that Jesus should be given a chance to defend Himself (John 7:50–51). When the Pharisees claimed that none of them had chosen to follow Jesus, Nicodemus did not confess to being a follower. So, either he was still seeking or he was following Jesus in secret. But after Jesus's death, Nicodemus brought about seventy-five pounds' worth of myrrh and aloe to anoint His body (John 19:39–42). He and Joseph of Arimathea wrapped and buried Him in Joseph's tomb. John writes that Joseph of Arimathea was a disciple of Jesus, but a secret one for fear of the Jews (John 19:38). The assumption is that the same was true of Nicodemus.

In this initial story, Nicodemus was curious but didn't want people to know, so he came at night. It seems like he was legitimately curious for his own personal faith. If he had wanted to challenge Jesus, he would have done it publicly, as many of the other Pharisees did. But he really was intrigued. He saw something different in Jesus and wanted to find out for himself if He was the real deal. It is quite significant that Nicodemus would come to Jesus right after this public standoff in the temple. The leaders were beginning to oppose Jesus, and Nicodemus wanted to find out more before he went along with them.

Nicodemus said he *knew* Jesus was "a teacher from God" (v. 2), yet he struggled to believe His teaching, exclaiming, "How can these things be?" (v. 9). Nicodemus wasn't one of those Gospel characters who met Jesus and immediately believed. He wrestled with it, like so many of us do. What Jesus said to him was different from what he had been taught his whole life: To enter the kingdom of God, he didn't have to do more good deeds, study harder, or rise higher on the social ladder. He had to be born again. A passive verb. There wasn't anything Nicodemus could do to enter the kingdom. It was something that had to *be done to him*.

It's always amazing to analyze which teachings Jesus chose to share with which people. Although the gospel never changes, the way Jesus presented it varied from person to person. When someone came to Him, Jesus knew exactly what each person needed to hear, how they needed to be challenged or shown grace or both. The rich young ruler needed to be challenged in the area of wealth (Luke 18:18–23). The woman caught in adultery needed to hear that she was not condemned (John 8:1–11). Simon the Pharisee needed to hear that he too was a sinner (Luke 7:36–49). Nicodemus needed to hear that he had to be born again.

As a Pharisee, a member of the Sanhedrin, Nicodemus would have been born into a prestigious Jewish family. Pedigree was important to Jews; they kept meticulous records of their genealogies, because the family you were born into determined your destiny. If you were born into a priestly family, you became a priest. If you were born into a carpenter's family, you became a carpenter. Nicodemus would have been proud of his noble birth.

Jesus said that none of that mattered. Just as the apostle Paul said of his own pedigree. If anyone had the right to brag about his pedigree and his religious works, Paul did. But about it all, he said, "I count everything as loss because of the surpassing worth of knowing Christ Jesus my Lord . . . and count them as rubbish, in order that I may gain Christ" (Philippians 3:7-8). In God's kingdom, it doesn't matter if you were born into a prestigious family in Jerusalem or a poor carpenter's family in Galilee—or even in Assyria or Babylon or Egypt. The status of your earthly family doesn't matter. What matters is your place in *God's* family. Our first birth doesn't matter. What matters is the second birth.

BORN AGAIN

"Born again" is a phrase our culture throws around a lot, perhaps without really understanding what it means theologically. Since Jimmy Carter used the term "born-again Christian" to describe himself in the 1974 election, it has become a category for political polls and statistics. When someone calls to ask survey questions about policy or voting, they often ask, "Are you a born-again Christian?" It's confusing to use it as an adjective like that, as if there are "born-again Christians" and just regular Christians. This is because, by definition, *every* Christian is born again. Being born again is not a second step of the faith journey for people who are more serious about their faith. If you have not been born again, you are not a Christian.

"Born again" literally translates as "born from above," referring specifically to the heavenly realm. We see Jesus explaining this in verses 12–13. These are heavenly things, and Jesus understands them because He is from heaven. We already know from John's introduction in chapter 1 that Jesus was from above and He came down to earth to dwell with us. So, John's choice of language is deliberate here. Jesus is saying to His followers, "Just as I am 'from above,' you also must be 'from above.'"

The word for "born" in the phrase "born again" is the same Greek word used when Scripture calls Jesus the "only begotten" Son of God. The Nicene Creed is specific in its wording that Jesus was "begotten, not made." Born of the Father, but not physically *made* by Him. He exists with God forever in heaven—"from above." So, when Jesus talks about being born again here, being born "from above," He is not speaking of a literal physical birth but a spiritual one. Born again, begotten of the Spirit.

Nicodemus asks Jesus a somewhat obvious question here. "How can a man be born when he his old? Can he enter a second time into his mother's womb and be born?" Nicodemus is smart enough to know that a physical rebirth isn't possible, so Jesus must be talking on a spiritual level. He is being sarcastic. But the second time he asks, it seems to be a legitimate question, "How can these things be?"

This was typical for many people who met Jesus. They thought on a physical level and Jesus spoke on a spiritual level. The Jews expected the Messiah to rescue them from the Romans and reestablish the kingdom of Israel. His disciples didn't get it even when He explained it to them (Mark 8:31–38). Even after Jesus was resurrected, His disciples *still* believed Jesus's kingdom would be a physical one here on this earth (Acts 1:6). But when Pilate asked Jesus if he was really the king of the Jews, Jesus replied, "My kingdom is not of this world" (John 18:36). Jesus's kingdom is "from above."

In the age to come, the kingdom of God will be a physical kingdom where Jesus will rule on a physical throne. But in order for that to happen, the whole earth must be made new, because the kingdom of God is a kingdom without sin, death, crying, or pain (Revelation 21:4–5). But the kingdom of God is not *only* a future kingdom. Jesus didn't tell Pilate, "My kingdom will be . . ." He said, "My kingdom *is*." Because Christ defeated death through His resurrection, we can join that other-world kingdom now by being made new on a spiritual level.

Today, in the here and now, the kingdom of God is not a physical place. It is a *spiritual* kingdom composed of all of those from every earthly nation, tribe, and tongue who have been made new. When we become Christians, God "[delivers] us from the domain of darkness and [transfers] us to the kingdom of his beloved Son" (Colossians 1:13). We become citizens of God's kingdom, no matter which earthly kingdom we live in (Philippians 3:20). Jesus's kingdom is "from above," so in order to become citizens of His kingdom, we must be born "from above." We must be born from the Spirit so that we no longer belong to the world of darkness but to the new creation.

THE SPIRIT IS LIKE THE WIND

When Jesus compares the wind with the Spirit, the comparison is actually a play on words. In Greek, the word for "wind" and "spirit" are the same: *pneuma*. So in Greek, it reads, "The pneuma blows where it wishes. . . . So it is with everyone who is born of the *pneuma*." The Spirit is like the wind in that it "blows where it wishes," and even though you can hear its sound, "you do not know where it comes from or where it goes" (v. 8). We cannot control the Spirit or predict what the Spirit will do. We don't know when or where the Spirit will move in someone's life.

Elsewhere in the Gospel of John, Jesus said, "No one can come to me unless the Father who sent me draws him. . . . No one can come to me unless it is granted him by the Father" (John 6:44, 65). Even our faith is a gift from God, not our own work (Ephesians 2:8). We do not transform ourselves; we have to be transformed *by* God (Romans 12:2). We were dead in our trespasses and sins, and *God* made us alive in Christ (Ephesians 2:5). We could not do it to or for ourselves. We were dead! As Jesus says in that same passage in John, "It is the Spirit who gives life. The flesh is no help at all" (John 6:63). We cannot make ourselves be born again any more than we could make ourselves be born the first time. Birth is something that happens to *you*.

THE FLESH VERSUS THE SPIRIT

Jesus makes a sharp contrast here between flesh and Spirit. That which is born of the flesh is flesh, and that which is born of the Spirit is Spirit. Being born of the Spirit is completely different in nature from being born physically (birth by the flesh). When we are born again, we are not just changed or reformed. We are a completely new person—a new creation. The old has passed away (2 Corinthians 5:16–17). We were *dead* in our trespasses and sins and God *makes us alive* together with Christ (Ephesians 2:5). This new creation is not just the old creation cleaned up and made pretty, but an entirely new life.

When we are physically born of someone, we tend to be like that person. Biologically, we may get our father's nose or our mother's hair color. Environmentally, we may also inherit things from them—a good work ethic or a tendency to be late. If we are born of the Spirit, we will be like Him. We will bear the fruit of His Spirit—love, joy, peace, patience, kindness, goodness, faithfulness, gentleness, and self-control (Galatians 5:22–23). The fruit of the Spirit is intentionally called "fruit," because it is not something we can do by trying harder; as if by just working at it, we could be more loving or more peaceful. Instead, it is something the Spirit *produces* in us. And like fruit on a vine, it is something that grows over time.

The fruits of the Spirit are contrasted with the deeds of the flesh. By the flesh and the Spirit, the Bible doesn't mean our bodies versus our souls. It means our sinful human nature versus the Spirit, *God's* Spirit. In the first birth, our physical birth, we are born into the sinful human nature, original sin. What is natural for us is immorality, idolatry, and sinful desires. By nature, our hearts are "deceitful above all things, and desperately sick" (Jeremiah 17:9). We cannot follow God's law unless we are given a new spirit. Unless our hearts of stone are replaced with hearts of flesh (Jeremiah 31:31–34; Ezekiel 11:14–20).

But when we are made new, when we are born of the Spirit, we crucify "the flesh with its passion and desires" (Galatians 5:24), and we are able to be "led by the Spirit" (Galatians 5:18). We are no longer slaves to sin. We have been set free (Romans 6:17–18). This doesn't mean that once we are born from above, we will never struggle with sin again. But because the Spirit is in us, we are now *able* to walk by the Spirit. Just as a baby has to learn to walk and talk, when we are born again, we have to learn to walk and talk spiritually. How to live a new life in Christ. We are born a new creation, but we also grow in spiritual maturity (Ephesians 4:11–14).

When we become Christians, we are declared holy before God—what theologians call "justification" (1 Corinthians 1:30; 6:11). So we are holy, but we also *grow* in holiness throughout our lives. The Spirit continues to work in us, making us more and more like Jesus—what theologians call "sanctification" (2 Corinthians 3:18; Ephesians 4:13;

Hebrews 5:12–14; 6:1; 12:14; 1 Peter 2:2; 2 Peter 1:5–8). Sanctification is a journey that continues throughout our entire lives. We are never finished with it this side of heaven. We have been made a new creation, *and* we are "being transformed into his image with ever-increasing glory" (2 Corinthians 3:18). Then when we die, rise again, and enter the consummated kingdom of God, our transformation will be complete—what theologians call "glorification" (1 Corinthians 15:50–58). All of this is part of being made new. All of it is the work of the Spirit and not of ourselves.

Jesus makes such a stark contrast between flesh and Spirit, because those who are born from above will live different lives from those who are still living in the flesh. Their lives will look different, because they are citizens of another world. Those who still walk by the flesh set their mind on earthly things. Their "god is their belly" and "their end is destruction" (Philippians 3:17–21). But those who have been born again "seek the things that are above, where Christ is" (Colossians 3:1). If your life doesn't look any different from those of the flesh around you, then you haven't been born of the Spirit.

When you are born from above, your desires change, your perspective changes, and your reason for living changes. It's not behavior modification; it's a heart transplant. You don't just try harder to do better. You are changed from the inside out. You want to live for Jesus. You want to follow His ways. You want to walk by the Spirit. You want to seek the things above. Although you still have the same physical body, you are a completely new person.

QUESTIONS FOR REFLECTION

1. Describe your life before you were born again. How is your life different now?

2. In what ways can we still walk in the flesh as a Christian?

3. What does it look like practically to have the fruit of the Spirit in our lives? Give specific examples.

4. Look back on your life since you became a Christian. How has God grown you over time?

5. The Bible makes it clear that all of this is the work of the Spirit in us. So then what responsibility do we have?

6. Knowing that the Spirit blows where it wills, how can you pray for friends and family who have not been born again?

READ JOHN 3:14–21

GOD SO LOVED THE WORLD

Jesus makes it clear that the motivation for all of this is love. God's great love for the world. Not just those who have the right pedigree or the most checkmarks on their good-deeds record, but the whole world. Jesus did not come to condemn the world but to save it. God gave His Son for the world. Elsewhere, John wrote that this is the very definition of love—that God loved us and sent His son to die for us (1 John 4:10). Paul wrote that God showed His love for us in that Christ died for us *while we were still sinners* (Romans 5:8)—before we were born again, before we were new creations. Before we were washed, sanctified, and justified (1 Corinthians 6:11). We did nothing to deserve it, nothing to earn it. He did it because He loved us.

Jesus uses the word *whoever* four times in this passage: whoever believes, whoever believes, whoever believes, whoever does what is true (vv. 15, 16, 18, 21). Jesus's point here goes back to that first point He made with Nicodemus. It's not about your family tree or your social status or your list of accomplishments: *whoever* believes will not perish. Our human categories and rankings don't determine whether someone is good enough to enter the kingdom of God.

LIGHT AND DARKNESS

Jesus brings in another contrast—that of light and darkness. This reference to darkness would have struck Nicodemus much more than it does us who read it, because he had come to Jesus at night, under cover of darkness. Jesus repeats what we heard from John in chapter 1, that light has come into the world—Jesus, the light of the world. That light has come into the world to save the world. To call men "out of the darkness into His marvelous light" (1 Peter 2:9). To deliver them "from the domain of darkness" (Colossians 1:13). Whoever follows Jesus "will not walk in darkness but will have the light of life" (John 8:12).

But people love the darkness. By nature, in the flesh, we love the darkness. But when the Spirit makes us a new creation, He gives us a new heart. It changes what we love. We are able to love God, and we are able to love the light. Paul writes, "At one time you were darkness, but now you are light in the Lord. Live as children of the light" (Ephesians 5:8). He does not say, "Live this way because it is the right thing to do." Or, "Live this way to *become* children of the light." He says to live as the children of the light that you *already* are! God has saved you through Christ and brought you into the light. He has given you a new life! Now *live* in that new life. In the new life, in the rebirth, we can finally live the way we were meant to live! Jesus doesn't just bring eternal life; He also brings abundant life in the here and now (John 10:10).

Paul in Ephesians compares our lives before Christ to walking in the darkness and our coming to know Him as arising from the dead (5:14). In the flesh, people think they are happy in the darkness, in their sin. But knowing Christ, the light of the world, is like rising from the dead, waking from a deep sleep, and finally seeing the world for real. Imagine it's the most beautiful sunny day you've ever seen. The sky is brilliant blue, the sun is warming your face, and the top of your head even tingles because the sun shines on you. Having the light of Christ is like that sunny day, but infinitely better.

We weren't meant to live in darkness. We were meant to live in the light. For a while, maybe the darkness seemed like a fun place to be. But when the light finally shines on us, we can see just how awful the darkness was. That is what it is like to be made a new creation. Like rising from the dead. Like waking up from a deep sleep. Finally stepping out of darkness into the light. Jesus came to save the world. He came to bring people out of darkness into the light.

QUESTIONS FOR REFLECTION

1. Examine this metaphor of light. What is light like? What does it do? What does it bring? How does this help us understand Jesus more? How does it help us understand how the Spirit works in our lives?

2. Jesus said that light exposes the works of darkness. What things in your life were exposed as darkness once you became a Christian?

3. How is it an act of great love when God exposes our darkness?

4. How would you talk about Jesus, the light of the world, to someone who is still living in darkness?

READ JOHN 3:22–36

JESUS IS ABOVE ALL

This last section of the chapter may seem somewhat unrelated, but at the end, John really connects the previous two sections together. He uses the same phrase from the first section, "from above," to declare that Jesus is above all, and he repeats again the same statement from John 3:16, that *whoever* believes in Him has eternal life.

Jesus is not just a man. He is above all men—in authority and in nature. He is the One God has sent from heaven. There is no one like Jesus. In Him, God gave "His Spirit without measure" (v. 34). Jesus has the fullness of God's Spirit dwelling in Him. God gives believers His Spirit when they become a new creation, but Jesus *is* God. Jesus speaks the very words of God (v. 34). He speaks truth, and yet people don't believe it. It harkens back to what Jesus said to Nicodemus in the first section—you are supposed to be a *teacher* of Israel, and yet you don't understand these things? The things Jesus was saying were foretold by the prophets, and yet the teachers of Israel did not accept it.

Their hearts were hardened. They loved the darkness. They claimed to know and love and follow God, but they didn't even recognize Him when He came to them in the flesh (John 8:18–19).

So, at the end of this chapter, where Nicodemus has struggled with whether or not to believe Jesus, John the Baptist declares that Jesus is the Christ. Then the Gospel writer John declares it all to be true as well. Remember the purpose of John's book? "That you may believe that Jesus is the Christ, the Son of God, and that by believing, you may have life in His name" (John 20:31). John wants to be sure we know that Jesus is the Christ and that believing in Him brings eternal life. He does not leave us with Nicodemus's question, "How can these things be?" He answers it through the voice of John the Baptist, "A person cannot receive even one thing unless it is given him from heaven" (v. 27). Faith is a gift from God. Salvation is a gift from God. New life is a gift from God. Sanctification is a gift from God. All of it comes as a gift from heaven.

John the Baptist compares himself to a groomsman at a wedding—not the "main event," but there to point ahead to the groom. John came only to prepare the way for Jesus. John knows his place in God's plan. "He must increase, but I must decrease" (v. 30). John declares that his joy is now complete because Jesus is here in the flesh. Jesus is ministering and bringing people into fellowship with the Father. With John the Baptist, we can rejoice at all Jesus does in our lives, and at all the Spirit does. We can point to Him, not to ourselves. It's not about us; it's about Him. He must increase; we must decrease.

QUESTIONS FOR REFLECTION

1. How would you describe how the Spirit works in our lives to someone who has not yet been reborn?

2. What would it look like for you to point others to Jesus with your life? How would you live differently?

3. What new insights have you gained after studying this chapter? How could they be applied to your life?

ON THE LAST DAY OF THE FEAST,

THE GREAT DAY, JESUS STOOD

UP AND CRIED OUT, "IF ANYONE THIRSTS,

LET HIM COME TO ME AND DRINK.

WHOEVER BELIEVES IN ME,

AS THE SCRIPTURE HAS SAID,

'OUT OF HIS HEART WILL FLOW

RIVERS OF LIVING WATER.'"

—

JOHN 7:37-38

LIVING WATER

READ JOHN 4:1–42

This week's story relates another personal encounter between Jesus and an unexpected person. But someone completely different from last week's character. We see again how Jesus uses different metaphors for different people in different situations to meet people where they are, to speak their language, and to share the gospel.

SAMARIA

At this point in the story, the Pharisees had learned of Jesus's success, which caused Him to withdraw into Galilee until it was time for His sacrifice. The quickest way to get from Jerusalem to Galilee, which took three days, was to go through Samaria. But the strictest Jews, including the Pharisees from whom He was escaping, took a longer route to avoid the Samaritans because Jews did not associate with Samaritans. Because the Samaritans had intermarried with Gentiles, Jews considered them to be half-breeds. The sharp divide between Jews and Gentiles began when the remnant of Israel returned from Babylon after the exile. While Nehemiah was rebuilding the walls of Jerusalem, Sanballat, the leader of the Samaritans, vehemently opposed him (Nehemiah 2:9–20; 6:1–14). The Samaritans built their own place of worship on Mount Gerizim along with their own priesthood and rituals.

So when John says Jesus "had to" go through Samaria, He most likely meant that God had a spiritual reason for Him to go that way, not that he *had* to geographically. John emphasizes that He "had to" go through Samaria to show that, in order to meet with an outsider, Jesus intentionally defied what the religious leaders of His day considered appropriate. Jesus doesn't avoid Samaria. He intentionally goes *into* Samaria. Because if wanted to reach the Samaritans, He *had* to go to Samaria. Jesus doesn't just wait for people to come to Him. He seeks out the lost (Luke 19:10).

THE SAMARITAN WOMAN

In the last lesson, we noted that Jesus speaks the same truth to different people in different ways. The gospel never changes, but the *way* He shared it could change based on the person He was trying to reach. That these two stories, of the Samaritan woman and Nicodemus, are back to back in John's Gospel emphasizes how different these two characters are and how differently Jesus speaks to them. Both receive the same basic message, the gospel. Both messages have an emphasis on the Spirit. But the messages use different metaphors, different language, and different background information. In this story, we see that both geographically and spiritually, Jesus met the Samaritan woman where she was.

The Samaritan woman was as different from Nicodemus as she could be. He was an educated, orthodox Jewish man, an influential leader among the elite class of Pharisees. She was an unknown Samaritan woman—she isn't even named in the text. And not only that, she had such a reputation as a sinner that she was shunned by her own community. She went to gather water in the heat of the day to avoid seeing anyone else at the local well. We don't know exactly why she had had five husbands and the man she was currently with was not her husband, but that little bit of backstory gives us a glimpse into why she would be avoiding community. There was no reason Jesus should have even talked to her. She had three strikes against her:

→ Jews did not associate with Samaritans.
→ Men did not talk with women who were not their wives, and certainly not about spiritual things like theology and worship.
→ Upright, moral people did not associate with known sinners.

Jesus knew all about her reputation and still reached out to her. He sought her out. And He broke all the rules to do it. He asked her for water, which would have meant drinking from a Samaritan vessel, which Jews would have considered unclean. Jesus asking this woman for a drink of water would be like searching for a homeless person today and asking for a swig from their canteen.

She was a nobody, an outcast. Yet Jesus reached out to her. He treated her with respect. He let her know that He knew about her past and still wanted to talk with her. He didn't shame her. Instead, He spoke kindly to her. He showed respect for her intellect and her spirituality. He listened to her and shared deep spiritual truths with her. In the Gospel of John, she was the first person to whom Jesus revealed that He was the Messiah.

And she was the first evangelist in the Gospel of John. This unknown sinner, this outcast, this Samaritan woman was the first person we see going to the rest of her town and telling them about Jesus. Again, she had several strikes against her:

→ In their culture, the testimony of a woman was considered so unreliable that it wasn't accepted in court.
→ She was an outcast in her community because of her status as a sinner.
→ She didn't really understand the intricacies of theology; she just knew there was something about Jesus.

Yet when she met Jesus and realized who He was, she left her water jar and hurried into town to tell everyone she saw about Him. She didn't hesitate. She didn't stop to ask herself whether anyone would believe her. She didn't even finish her chores. She was so impacted by her encounter with Jesus that she had to tell everyone. And the text says, "Many Samaritans from that town believed in Him *because of the woman's testimony*" (v. 39; emphasis added). Although we may glaze over that part today, it would have been absolutely shocking in their culture that anyone listened to, much less believed, her testimony. But the Spirit was at work shattering barriers and turning the religious world upside down. While the upstanding Jewish religious leaders were feeling threatened by Jesus's growing power, those despised by society were coming to Him in faith.

QUESTIONS FOR REFLECTION

1. What do you learn about Jesus's character from His interaction with the Samaritan woman?

2. What other times in Scripture does Jesus reach out to those who are outcast or marginalized?

3. What kinds of barriers has our culture created between people? Why?

4. How can we reach out to those who are outcasts in our society? How can we treat them the way Jesus would?

5. How can we learn from believers who are different from us? Those who may have come from a different background? Those who have been through different struggles?

READ JOHN 7:38–39

LIVING WATER

"Living water" was a common expression for any flowing water, like a river or stream, as distinct from still water, like the water of well. Living water was fresher, cleaner, and more satisfying than water from a cistern or a well. So the Samaritan woman's question is not ignorant. It would have been totally appropriate. But as John always does, he uses a play on words—"living water" doesn't just mean water that is flowing; it means the water that brings life.

Water was a prominent symbol in the Old Testament. In a land that was quite dry, water was a valuable commodity. Entire civilizations were built around access to fresh, clean water. Towns or villages were built around wells. Water was often used as a symbol for life because it is literally the most basic thing we need to survive. You can live three weeks without food, but only three days without water. These essential needs—food and water—create the perfect metaphors for what Jesus provides. Jesus satisfies our deepest needs, our deepest hungers, our deepest thirsts.

In this passage, although Jesus said He would give her the living water, later at the Feast of the Tabernacles He said He *is* the living water (John 7). Which is it? He does the same thing with the imagery of the bread (John 6). He fed them bread and then said He *is* the bread from heaven. He even brought the two metaphors together. "I am the bread of life; whoever comes to me shall not hunger, and whoever believes in me shall never thirst" (John 6:35).

When the Israelites wandered through the wilderness in the Old Testament, God supernaturally provided food and water for them. He literally made bread rain from the heavens (Exodus 16) and made water flow out of a rock (Exodus 17). In John 6, Jesus said He is the true bread from heaven, because He came down from heaven to give life to the world (John 6:33, 41). Instead of just keeping us alive here on earth, He gives us eternal life in heaven. In the same way, He is the water that brings eternal life. There is no need to go back for refills. When you drink from this water, you will never thirst again.

ALL WHO ARE THIRSTY

Thousands of years before Christ, Isaiah understood that God is the source of this living water, the One who quenches our thirst. He wrote that the Lord will "satisfy your desire in scorched places and give strength to your bones. And you will be like a watered garden and like a spring of water whose waters do not fail" (Isaiah 58:11). Jeremiah calls God "the fountain of living waters" (Jeremiah 2:13; 17:13). The psalmist wrote poetically of our spiritual thirst for God:

> O God, you are my God; earnestly I seek you;
> my soul thirsts for you, my flesh faints for you,
> as in a dry and weary land where there is no water. (Psalm 63:1)

> I stretch out my hands to you;
> My soul longs for you, as a parched land. (Psalm 143:6)

> As the deer pants for flowing streams so my soul pants for you, O God. (Psalm 42:1)

The imagery here is strong. Our soul thirsts for God. We have a deep, longing thirst that nothing else can satisfy. And God invites all who are thirsty to come and drink their fill. All who are hungry to come and be satisfied (Isaiah 55:1–4). Not just with bread and water, but with rich food and abundance. Jesus invites all—the unknown, outcast Samaritan woman and the respected, upright religious leader Nicodemus. All who are thirsty. Everyone is invited to come, eat, drink, and enjoy.

When Jesus proclaimed that He was the living water in John 7, it was at a pivotal moment in the Feast of Tabernacles, which celebrated the time that Israel lived in the wilderness. Water was especially prominent in this feast—the third daily ceremony was the rite of the water libation. On the first morning of the festival, a procession of priests went down to the pool of Siloam to bring up to the temple a golden container with enough water to last for the seven days of the festival. The water was brought up with great ceremony. The *shofar*—a ram's horn trumpet—was blown, the people waved palm branches, and the priests carried the water around the altar as psalms were recited. Then each day, the priest poured out the contents of two silver bowls—one of water, one of wine. This was an expression of dependence on God to pour out His blessing of rain upon the earth. One the last day of the feast, the water libation reached its climax in a ceremony called the *Hoshana Rabbah*, the "Great Hosanna," which translates "save us now!" On this day, they walked around the altar seven times and poured out the rest of the water with great pomp and ceremony.

At this exact moment in the festival, Jesus stood up and cried with a loud voice, "If anyone thirsts, let him come to me and drink. Whoever believes in me, as the Scripture has said, 'Out of his heart will flow rivers of living water'" (John 7:38). Jesus definitely wasn't hiding any more. This was as public a proclamation as you could get. Jesus was claiming to be the One who saves us. The One who quenches our thirst. The One who brings us eternal life. He was claiming to be God Himself.

To the Samaritan woman, Jesus said, "The water that I will give him will become in him a spring of water welling up to eternal life" (John 4:14). Without Christ, you will always be thirsty. You will never be satisfied. But in Christ, the river flows and your thirst is quenched.

This offer is for all who believe—Jew, Greek, Samaritan. Man, woman, child. Priests and outcasts, royalty and fishermen. The first person to whom Jesus proclaims Himself to be the living water was a Samaritan woman, someone whom Jewish men may have considered as good as a wild dog (Matthew 7:6). Yet from the beginning, in the Old Testament, the living water was for all. Yes, God provided in the wilderness for His chosen people, but He also provided water in the wilderness for Hagar and Ishmael, the nonchosen ones (Genesis 21:19). The arms-open-wide Jesus of the New Testament is the same opens-open-wide God of the Old Testament:

→ "Come, everyone who thirsts, come to the waters" (Isaiah 55:1).
→ "Come to me and drink" (John 7:37; emphasis added).

QUESTIONS FOR REFLECTION

1. What kinds of things do we hunger and thirst after?

2. What does that hunger and thirst reveal about our deeper needs?

3. How would you say Jesus satisfies your spiritual thirst?

4. Is there any area of your life where you feel hungry or thirsty? Explain your answer.

5. Is there any way you could feel more satisfied, more at peace, more content?

READ JOHN 4:16–26 AGAIN

WORSHIP IN SPIRIT AND IN TRUTH

The beginning of the conversation between Jesus and this woman is metaphorical. He starts the conversation by asking her for a drink of water, using the request as an opening to talk about the true living water. Then, in verse 16, Jesus quickly turns the conversation very personal, letting her know that He knows about her past. He knows her intimately. He knows so much about her, in fact, that she believes Him to be a prophet.

So now *she* turns the conversation and asks Him a question. It shifts from very personal to theological debate pretty fast. Perhaps she was embarrassed or didn't want him to dig deeper. Maybe she was just trying to change the subject. Or just maybe, she realized she had an expert here, and she really wanted to know the answers to her burning questions. It is actually quite telling that the conversation goes this way. This Samaritan woman, this sinner, this outcast, figures out that Jesus is a prophet and she doesn't ask Him about her future or for His blessing. She asks Him about the right way to worship.

The location of the well where Jesus met the Samaritan woman, Jacob's well, is still well known and included in tours of the Holy Land. It is within view of Mount Gerizim, which was holy to the Samaritans—"this mountain" to which the Samaritan woman refers (v. 20). Right beside it is Mount Ebal, and between the two mountains was the city of Shechem, the location of Jacob's well. In Deuteronomy, when the Israelites entered the promised land, they pronounced the blessings of the covenant on Mount Gerizim and the curses of the covenant on Mount Ebal (Deuteronomy 11:29). The Samaritans worshiped on Mount Gerizim because it was the place of blessing. They did not recognize Jerusalem and the temple as the place of worship because the temple was not established until the time of the monarchy, in the book of Kings. The Samaritans recognized only the first five books—the Pentateuch—as Scripture. This was the most pressing issue between Samaritans and Jews—where to worship, which place to consider sacred.

Ancient cultures were committed to holy sites. They believed holiness to be a tangible thing, related to places and objects—the temple, the ark of the covenant, etc. The Jews believed God's Spirit physically dwelt in the temple, in the Holy of Holies, between the cherubim on the mercy seat of the Ark of the Covenant. The Spirit is what made that space the "Holy of Holies" or the "Most Holy Place." God's Spirit dwelling among them is what made Israel a holy nation.

But Jesus tells the Samaritan woman that soon, it really won't matter *where* they worship, because God's Spirit will no longer be contained to the Holy of Holies, behind the veil (Matthew 27:51). The Spirit will be poured out on all believers—male and female, old and young (Acts 2:17). God's Spirit will dwell in the hearts of those who believe, and they will become temples themselves (1 Corinthians 6:19). You won't have to go to the temple to meet with God. He will be with you all the time and everywhere you go (John 16). In fact, that time is even now here (John 4:23), because Christ Himself was filled with God's Spirit and carried God's Spirit with Him. So, the Samaritan woman was "at the temple" right then because she was meeting with Jesus.

Throughout the whole Old Testament, God criticized the people's worship when their hearts weren't in it. When they did all the right "stuff"—the feasts, the sacrifices, the prayers—but their hearts were far from Him, God said, "I hate, I despise your feasts, and I take no delight in your solemn assemblies" (Amos 5:21). God said true fasting is "to loose the bonds of wickedness, to undo the straps of the yoke, to let the oppressed go free . . . to share your bread with the hungry and bring the homeless poor into your house" (Isaiah 58:6–7).

True worship isn't about where you offer your sacrifices, but where your heart is. After his sin with Bathsheba, David wrote, "You will not delight in sacrifice, or I would give it; you will not be pleased with a burnt offering. The sacrifices of God are a broken spirit; a broken and contrite heart, O God, you will not despise" (Psalm 51:16–17). Worship can be expressed in any way and in any place, but true worship is an issue of the heart. True spiritual worship is when we offer all of us, our whole lives, as a living sacrifice (Romans 12:1).

So, it doesn't matter *where* we worship—on a mountain, in a temple or sanctuary, on the streets, or in our homes—but that we worship in spirit and in truth. In spirit—that we are born again, born of the Spirit, that the Holy Spirit is in our hearts. And truth—that our hearts are worshiping the true God, submitting to the truth of the gospel of Jesus, who is the way, the truth, and the life (John 14:6).

QUESTIONS FOR REFLECTION

1. What keeps us from offering God all of ourselves as a living sacrifice?

2. Are there any ways your heart needs to change in your worship? How could you make those changes?

3. Are there any areas in your life that you need to give to God in submission? How can you do that?

4. What's one practical thing you can do this week to worship God from the heart?

5. Worship is not just what we do on Sundays, but how we live our whole lives. How will you worship God and live by His truth throughout your week?

JESUS SAID TO HER, "I AM THE
RESURRECTION AND THE LIFE. WHOEVER
BELIEVES IN ME, THOUGH HE DIE, YET
SHALL HE LIVE, AND EVERYONE WHO
LIVES AND BELIEVES IN ME SHALL
NEVER DIE. DO YOU BELIEVE THIS?"

———

JOHN 11:25-26

I AM *the* RESURRECTION

JOHN 11 AND 14

READ JOHN 11:1-5

LAZARUS, MARY, AND MARTHA

The opening verses of this passage give us some details on who the characters in this encounter with Jesus were and how close they were to Jesus. Lazarus's sisters send for Jesus with the words, "Lord, he whom you love is ill" (John 11:3). This was certainly a statement of intimacy, similar to the title John used when he referred to himself as "the disciple whom Jesus loved." Two more times in this story, John specifically mentions Jesus's great love for Lazarus and his sisters (John 11:5, 36). While this story teaches us a deep theological truth and contains the biggest miracle of His ministry besides His own resurrection, it is also a very personal story of Jesus and three people whom He deeply loved.

This was the same Mary, Martha, and Lazarus who hosted Jesus and the disciples on several other occasions. Specifically, John mentions when Mary anointed Jesus's feet with perfume and wiped His feet with her hair, which in the book of John actually happens *after* this story—one chapter later (John 12:1-8). Yet as the narrator, John can still refer to this event, assuming his audience knew about it, even though they hadn't yet read it in his Gospel.

The other well-known story of Jesus at their house was when Jesus praised Mary for sitting at His feet and listening to His teaching, and told Martha that her worry about the physical duties of hosting (cleaning, cooking, etc.) was distracting her from what was really important (Luke 10:38-42). Many have criticized Martha for being a worrier or shallow, but she was doing what any woman of a household would be expected to do for any visitor, much less a visitor as important as Jesus. Hospitality was a sacred value in biblical times.

What Mary did would have been radical for a woman, even scandalous or inappropriate. Sitting at the feet of a rabbi was reserved for the most serious of his disciples, those preparing to become rabbis themselves. Women were not permitted to become rabbis at that time. They could listen to a rabbi's teaching in the synagogues, but they would not typically be allowed to sit at his feet like a disciple. This is why Martha felt so confident when she told Jesus to tell Mary to help her—she knew she was in the right. But Jesus, as He always did, flipped the world's categories and norms on their heads. Just like in the last lesson when He discussed theological issues with a Samaritan woman, even a known sinner. In this story, He did it again by welcoming a woman into His group of disciples.

Jesus wasn't telling Martha that hospitality wasn't important (we see Martha serving dinner again in John 12:2), but that her relationship with Him was the most important thing. Jesus didn't criticize Martha's hospitality or serving, only her worry and anxiety about those things. Just as He taught in the Sermon on the Mount, "Do not be anxious about your life, what you will eat or what you will drink, nor about your body, what you will put on. . . . But seek first the kingdom of God and his righteousness, and all these things will be added to you" (Matthew 6:25-33).

It is very likely that these three siblings hosted Jesus and His disciples in their home many times, perhaps even every time He came to Bethany. These are close, personal friends of Jesus, not strangers. People Jesus deeply loved. People He considered disciples, though they weren't of the Twelve.

READ JOHN 11:6-17

THE GLORY OF GOD

When Lazarus fell ill, Mary and Martha sent for Jesus, hoping—maybe even assuming—Jesus would come to heal him. They both said to Jesus, "If you had been here, Lazarus wouldn't have died." But Jesus told His disciples that the purpose of this illness was "for the glory of God, so that the Son of God [Himself] may be glorified through it" (v. 4). And "I am glad that I was not there, so that you may believe" (v. 15). Jesus said something similar to His disciples when they asked about the man who had been born blind—that this happened so "the works of God might be displayed in him" (John 9:3). This man was born blind so Jesus could heal him and people would see it and believe. Lazarus died so that Jesus could raise him from the dead and people would see it and believe.

Jesus waited two days before leaving for Bethany. When He arrived, Lazarus would have been in the tomb for four days. By then, the body would have started to decompose enough to smell. The human body starts to bloat, and blood-containing foam leaks from the mouth and nose. In other words, no one would be able to argue that Lazarus wasn't really dead. Jesus was making sure this miracle would be irrefutable.

Jesus told the disciples that Lazarus's illness "does not lead to death" (v. 4) and yet a few verses later, He told them, "Lazarus has died" (v. 14). Though Lazarus did die from this illness, that was not the end of the story. His death led to life, just as our deaths will one day lead to eternal life. If Lazarus had not died, he could not have been resurrected. In the same way, Jesus Himself had to die in order to be raised again—to accomplish the sacrifice for sin, conquer death, and bring eternal life. This miracle is a foreshadowing of the death and resurrection of Jesus Himself, which brings us eternal life.

QUESTIONS FOR REFLECTION

1. Why is it significant that Jesus loved these people and had a personal relationship with them? What does this tell you about Jesus?

2. How have you seen the glory of God displayed through difficult times, either in your life or the lives of others?

3. In what ways can we find ourselves getting distracted from the "most important thing" of sitting at the feet of Jesus? What worries or anxieties keep us from spending time with Jesus?

READ JOHN 11:17-27

MARTHA

In this story, it was Martha who went out to meet Jesus, even though it was Mary who may have seemed closer to Jesus in the other stories. Martha, the practical one. But still one with great faith. Martha said, "Lord, if you had been here, my brother would not have died" (v. 21). We don't know if she said it desperately through tears, accusatorily in anger, or a mix of both. Most likely, she had a range of emotions, but she probably thought, at least in part, "Come on, Jesus. Why didn't you save him? I know you loved him!" She had no doubt in Jesus Himself and His power, because she also said, "But even now I know that whatever you ask from God, God will give you" (v. 22). Martha didn't doubt *Him*, but she questioned His plan. Like we often do. We assume that if God really loved us, He would keep bad things from happening to us. We can't see the bigger plan; that sometimes it is *through* the bad things that Jesus is most glorified (v. 4). If Jesus hadn't let Lazarus die, He wouldn't have been able to raise him.

So, Jesus had a theological discussion with Martha, the one who *hadn't* been sitting at His feet that day. The one He encouraged to focus on discipleship. Not because Martha didn't believe and needed to be convinced. But because she *did* believe. She had the faith, but He was going to give her the theology. Just as He had explained real worship to the woman at the well, Jesus explained resurrection to Martha.

I AM THE RESURRECTION AND THE LIFE

Jesus told her Lazarus would rise again. She answered she knew he would rise again in the resurrection on the last day. But Jesus told her, "*I am* the resurrection and the life." Not just that *He brings* resurrection, but that He is the resurrection. Like He had told them He was the bread of life that came down from heaven in the Exodus (John 6:35), the living water spoken of in the Feast of Booths (John 7:38), the Good Shepherd written about in Psalms (John 10:11).

It is truly amazing that Jesus spoke this significant "I Am" statement privately, to one person, and that person was a woman. And a rather insignificant woman by the world's standards. The first person He explicitly told He was the Messiah was a woman—a Samaritan woman, a sinner, an outcast (John 4). It was another insignificant woman, Mary Magdalene, to whom He first revealed Himself after His resurrection (John 20). It cannot be coincidence that throughout the book of John, Jesus reveals these major theological truths to women, and in private, just to the two of them. For these truths to be passed along, these women would have to tell others, but in their culture, the testimony of women was not trusted. Jesus was absolutely revolutionary in the way He treated women.

Jesus explains to Martha, "I am the resurrection and the life. Whoever believes in me will live, though he die, yet shall he live, and everyone who lives and believes in me shall never die" (John 11:25–26). This sounds like a riddle. Even if we die, we will live? When we studied what it means to be born again, we learned that there are two births, a physical birth and a spiritual birth. Scripture says there are also two deaths, a physical death and a spiritual death. The book of Revelation calls the spiritual death the "second death," the lake of fire (Revelation 2:11; 20:6, 14–15). We who have been born again may die a physical death, but we will not die the spiritual death. That spiritual birth is eternal. Though we will all die physically, those of us who believe in Jesus will not die spiritually. We will live forever. So even though we will die, we will never *really* die.

After He explained this, Jesus asked Martha point blank, "Do you believe this?" She had already said she believed, even before He started talking theology with her. So why did He ask if she believed? Her answer gives us a clue. She didn't say "Yes, Lord, I believe in the theological concept of resurrection and eternal life." She said, "Yes, Lord. I believe in *you*."

It wasn't just about her intellectual or theological belief. Ultimately, it was about her belief *in Him*. Her trust in Him. In the Bible, faith is not just intellectual belief in a concept or a theological argument. It is trust in a person. Jesus didn't just bring resurrection and life; He is the resurrection and the life. Jesus doesn't just show us the way. He is the way. Jesus was asking, "Do you trust Me? Even if things look grim right now, even if it looks like death? Do you have faith in Me that I have a plan? Are you willing to trust Me, to follow Me, wherever the path leads? Even if it means your brother's death? Do you trust that I have a bigger plan in mind?"

Martha was able to look at Jesus in the midst of her grief and say, "Yes, Lord. I believe in you." Yes, Lord, I trust in you. I trust in your plan. No matter what happens. Even unto death. I know you are the resurrection and the life. So, I know that even if my brother dies, even if I die, we have eternal life in you. Martha could not have been more on target theologically. Jesus wasn't just talking to one of His dearest friends; he was talking to one of His most devout disciples. Though earlier Jesus had chided her for being worried about physical things, here she got the "one thing" that really mattered—that Jesus was the Son of God, the Messiah. He was and is the resurrection and the life.

QUESTIONS FOR REFLECTION

1. If you had a formula or a product that could stop physical death, how would people in the world react?

2. Why don't people always have that same kind of reaction when we tell them about Jesus, the One who has the power to stop spiritual death, to bring eternal life?

3. Like Martha, do you sometimes struggle with understanding God's plan? How can we trust in Him even when it seems like things aren't going the way they should?

READ JOHN 11:28–37

MARY

When Mary came out to meet Jesus, He didn't offer another theological explanation. He wept with her. Even though He was about to raise Lazarus from the dead, Jesus wept. Because He saw Mary weeping and all the Jews weeping with her, He was "deeply moved in spirit and troubled" (v. 33). This was a deep, heart-wrenching kind of weeping. Jesus knew how the story would end, and still He joined them in their grief.

But His grief also had a sense of anger, which we can miss in the English. The Greek word here means to snort, with intense displeasure, anger, or indignation. Lazarus's death and the pain it caused those who loved him made Jesus angry. Death makes God angry. It was not part of His design. It is what happens because of sin. God hates death. That is why Jesus came to conquer death—to bring life!

God hates death so much that He Himself died to conquer it. He voluntarily went through the thing He hates in order to save us from it (Romans 5:14–21). As He said with another "I Am" statement, "I am the Good Shepherd." He came that we might have life and have it to the fullest (John 10:10). He brought us life by laying down His life for us (John 10:11). Because He loves us. This isn't just a theological passage; it is a story of Jesus's great love for His close friends. Lazarus's death made Jesus angry because He loved him so much. All death makes Jesus angry because He loves us so much.

READ JOHN 11:38–48

THE RESURRECTION

When Jesus commanded them to take away the stone, He prayed. In that prayer, He didn't ask God to raise Lazarus. He thanked God for already having heard His prayer, for already answering. Jesus knew God had already performed the miracle, but He thanked God aloud so the people standing nearby would believe He was from the Father (v. 42). Just as He had said to the disciples, so that the glory of God would be shown. So they would believe the Father had sent Him. Because God alone has the power over life and death, there could be no denying now that Jesus was sent from God. Jesus had done many signs and wonders, but raising someone from the dead took things to a whole new level. Even His enemies admitted that. They tried to devise a plan to stop Him because, as they said, "If we let him go on like this, everyone will believe in Him" (v. 48).

So Jesus proves now what He had said to Martha earlier—"I am the resurrection and the life." This is the ultimate object lesson. Jesus had said, "Whoever believes in me, though he die, yet he shall live." And then He shows them with Lazarus. Lazarus had died, and now he will live. The resurrection of Lazarus made their faith tangible. Belief in Jesus isn't a theoretical hope. It is a practical reality. The people saw Lazarus with their own eyes. They could touch him and speak with him. They knew it to be true. Jesus was who He said He was. The resurrection and the life.

QUESTIONS FOR REFLECTION

1. How does it make you feel to know that Jesus wept with Mary and the others, even though He knew the end of the story? How can this encourage you when you are upset?

2. Why are miracles still not enough for some to believe that Jesus is the Son of God?

3. How do you think Martha felt after hearing Jesus say He was the resurrection and the life, and then seeing Him raise Lazarus from the dead?

4. How does the truth that Jesus is the resurrection and the life affect your day-to-day life?

READ JOHN 14:1–11

I AM THE WAY, THE TRUTH, AND THE LIFE

In this passage, the disciples are at the Last Supper in the Upper Room. Jesus washed their feet and told them about Peter's denial and Judas's betrayal. Then He gave them His final instructions and reiterated His most important teachings, the things He really wanted them to remember. The very first thing He said was that they shouldn't fear, because when He left them, He was going to prepare a place for them in God's house, and they would follow Him later. Thomas, always the practical one, asked how they could know the way to where He was going. As if the way to heaven could be plotted out on a map. Jesus answered with another "I am" statement. Jesus doesn't just show people the way to heaven, He *is* the way. When the people asked Jesus to give them the bread and the water that would give them eternal life, He said, "*I am* the bread of life," and "*I am* the living water." It's not about what Jesus can give me; it's about who He is. Our faith isn't about what God can do for us; it's about a relationship with Him. In this passage Jesus says, "I am the way."

"No one comes to the Father except through [Jesus]" (v. 6). Our ultimate destination is the Father. This chapter has more references to the Father than any other chapter in Scripture. The way to God isn't a road or a path. It isn't even a religion or a way of doing life. It's Jesus Himself. The person of Jesus. It's not about all the stuff you do; it's about whether you know Jesus. It's not the law or our works or our theology that saves us. It's Jesus. Jesus didn't just come to show us the way to God. Jesus *is* God, come to earth. He didn't come just to tell us how to receive eternal life. He came and died so we *could* receive eternal life. He didn't come to show us the way. He came and died to *make* the way.

Jesus is the door of the sheep (John 10:7). He is the only way to the Father. He is the resurrection and the life. There is salvation in no one else (Acts 4:12). But this isn't an exclusive statement. Yes, Jesus is the only door, but that door is open to all. In the Father's house, there are *many* rooms (John 14:2). There is room for everyone. All who are thirsty can come and drink (Isaiah 55:1; John 7:37). God desires that all people be saved (1 Timothy 2:4; 2 Peter 3:9). This statement isn't arrogant or exclusive because, although Jesus is the only way, *everyone* is invited to come to Him (Matthew 11:28).

QUESTIONS FOR REFLECTION

1. How can you respond when people claim that saying "Jesus is the only way to heaven" is an exclusive statement?

2. What if you saw evangelism as an invitation to all—an *inclusive statement—welcoming them to come to Jesus and have a relationship with the Father through Him? How would that change the way you witness?*

3. In our pluralistic culture, how can we show respect other people's beliefs while standing firm in our belief that Jesus is the only way to heaven?

4. How has this week's lesson made you think differently about Jesus?

"A NEW COMMANDMENT I GIVE TO
YOU, THAT YOU LOVE ONE ANOTHER:
JUST AS I HAVE LOVED YOU, YOU
ALSO ARE TO LOVE ONE ANOTHER.
BY THIS ALL PEOPLE WILL KNOW THAT
YOU ARE MY DISCIPLES, IF YOU HAVE
LOVE FOR ONE ANOTHER."

—

JOHN 13:34-35

LOVE ONE ANOTHER
AS I HAVE LOVED YOU

READ JOHN 13:1–17

THE FEAST OF PASSOVER

This chapter opens with, "Now before the Feast of the Passover…" Passover was one of the three great pilgrim festivals of the Jewish year, along with Tabernacles and Pentecost. It is a seven-day festival in the spring that celebrates the barley harvest and the miraculous Passover event of the exodus. It is also called the Feast of Unleavened Bread to remind the Jews of their departure from Egypt, when they had to leave so quickly that they couldn't wait for their bread to rise (Exodus 12–14). In the Passover, the angel of death (the tenth plague on Egypt) passed over the houses of every Israelite who had covered their doorways with the blood of the Passover lamb.

The Passover meal had to be eaten within the walls of Jerusalem. Those who lived outside Jerusalem traveled to the city for the festival, so most homes included guests on the night of the feast. Representatives from each family would "prepare the Passover"—have the priests slaughter a lamb for them in the temple and then return with it for the Passover meal, to be eaten at sundown. The meal was often shared by two or more families shared the meal, since a minimum of ten people was required for the Passover meal. Here, Jesus and His closest disciples make up the family unit.

There is a discrepancy in the accounts about the timing of the Passover feast. According to Matthew, Mark, and Luke, Jesus ate the Passover with His disciples on Thursday night, but according to John, the priests planned to eat it on Friday night (John 18:28; 19:14). There are several explanations, the most popular are:

→   Several Jewish groups had different calendars and did not celebrate Passover on the same day because they disputed about when the month had begun, based on the moon.
→   Because of the high volume of lambs needed for all the Passover feasts around the city, the priests commanded some to celebrate it on Thursday and some on Friday.
→   The disciples celebrated a day early because Jesus knew what would happen to Him on Friday, but they did so without the lamb slaughtered in the temple.

Whether it was the actual Passover meal or the night before, the Gospels make a theological point of connection between Passover and Jesus's death as the new covenant's Passover lamb. The Gospels all call Jesus the Lamb of God, and Jesus Himself makes verbal connections during the meal. It was customary for the head of the household to give thanks for the bread and the wine before any meal, but special blessings were said over bread and wine at Passover. Over the Passover bread He said, "This is the bread of affliction our ancestors ate when they came from Egypt." Jesus's blessing of "This is my body" was a new interpretation of that blessing. Jesus was redefining Passover in light of His own sacrifice.

The image of Christ as the Passover Lamb, along with His washing the disciples' feet, paints Jesus as the Suffering Servant Messiah of Isaiah 53. Jesus made His point very clear—He did not come as a conquering king to overthrow Rome and bring back the golden age of the Davidic monarchy in Israel. He came as a servant to suffer and to die for His people.

QUESTIONS FOR REFLECTION

1.   Why is a sacrifice for sin necessary? What does that say about how God views sin?

2. Read Hebrews 10:1–18. How was Jesus's sacrifice similar to what was offered under the old covenant? How was it different?

3. What does it say about Jesus that He was willing to offer Himself as a sacrifice for the world?

4. What are some practical ways you can model Jesus's example of sacrifice? What sacrifices can you make for others out of love?

HUMILITY

Jesus washing His disciples' feet was a sign of unprecedented humility for a rabbi. Footwashing was the task of the lowliest servant in the household, not a respected rabbi. Removing His outer garments would also have been a sign of great humility. It is especially interesting that Jesus makes this gesture of humility during a meal, a time when people of this culture arranged their seating by rank and honor. While Jews did value humility, they also took great pride in social status and position. Rabbi Judah ha-Nasi was said to be so humble that he would do anything for others *except* relinquish his superior seating position at a meal.

Disciples normally served their teachers, but Jesus voluntarily took the role of a servant before His disciples. This would have been an absolutely revolutionary statement for any rabbi to make. In fact, Jesus's act violates cultural norms so much that Peter finds it unthinkable, even offensive—"You shall never wash my feet!" Peter's refusal to accept this service from Jesus would have seemed noble of him. It was meant as a sign of respect for Jesus's authority, His status as a rabbi, and even more so, as the Messiah, the Son of God. But in God's kingdom, social status and honor are turned upside down. Jesus answered, "If I do not wash you, you have no part with me." If we do not accept Christ's humble service and sacrifice for us, we have no part with Him.

Jesus, the Son of God, Creator of all things, King of kings and Lord of lords came down from His throne on high and voluntarily lived among us as one of us. He suffered and died at the hands of cruel men in the most horrible way imaginable (Philippians 2:1–8). He who knew no sin became sin on our behalf (2 Corinthians 5:21). The only One who has ever lived a perfect, sinless life, the One who did not deserve death died for me and for you. Jesus was the very picture of humility. He calls us to follow Him, to be like Him, to imitate Him, to do the same.

AS I HAVE DONE TO YOU

Meals provided common settings in which rabbis taught their disciples. In the book of John, this is Jesus's longest block of teaching, covering four entire chapters. This particular meal would have been a special time of teaching anyway because it was the Passover, but Jesus knew it was His last Passover. He knew it was His last night with them and that these were His final words to them. This is what Jesus wanted them to know most of all. This is what He wanted them to remember and live out when He was gone.

Disciples were to learn by imitating their teachers; not just learning what they said, but doing what they did. Jesus told them clearly that this was a time of teaching. After washing their feet, He resumed His place at the table and explained, "Do you understand what I have done to you? . . . I have given you an example, that you also should do just as I have done to you" (vv. 12–15). Not that they should literally go around washing everyone's feet, but that to really love someone is to serve them. Real love is sacrifice. Real love is giving of yourself for others.

Jesus calls us to go and do likewise. Go and live the way Jesus lived. Serve the way Jesus served. Love the way Jesus loved. Because what you do reveals what you really believe. Actions speak louder than words about who you really are on the inside. If you really know and love Jesus, you will love those He loved with a servant's heart. You will step down from whatever position of honor the world has given you, get down on your hands and knees, and wash feet. It is the highest honor we could have to serve others in the name of Christ.

QUESTIONS FOR REFLECTION

1. Read Philippians 2:1–8. What does this passage tell us about humility?

2. Do you know someone who does "footwashing" types of service, the lowly jobs with little glory? Consider examples you see in your community, church, or family.

3. What keeps us from lowering ourselves to do "footwashing" activities?

4. Think of a time when you went out of your way to serve someone. What did you learn from that experience?

5. What's one thing you can do this week to serve someone in your life?

READ JOHN 13:31–35

A NEW COMMANDMENT

In many denominations throughout the Church, the night of the Last Supper is often called "Maundy Thursday," from the Latin word for "mandate" or "commandment." Because, of everything Jesus said that night, this is the most important. This is what encompasses all that Jesus taught them that night—"Love as I have loved you." According to Jesus, this is the definition of what it means to be a disciple, how the world will know that we are His followers—if we love as He loved.

But it's strange to hear Jesus say this is a *new* commandment. Loving others isn't a new commandment. "Love your neighbor as yourself" is found way back when God first gave the Law to Moses (Leviticus 19:18). Jesus Himself even said all of the Law and the Prophets could be summed up by love—to love God and love others (Mark 12:30–31).

The Greek word here can mean fresh, novel, or innovative. Not necessarily a completely new idea, but an updated, "new and improved" version. The smartphone was a combination of two things that already existed, a computer and a phone, and yet was something completely new. This commandment was new in the same way. The love was not new, but the example of *how* to love was new.

Just a few chapters later, on the same night, Jesus repeated this commandment and followed it with, "Greater love has no one than this, that someone lay down his life for his friends" (John 15:12–13). It's not just "love your neighbor as yourself," but love others *as Christ loves you*. A footwashing, willing-to-die-for-you kind of love. Love so radically selfless that people will be shocked by it, just as Peter was that night.

This new commandment defines the new covenant Jesus instituted that night with His blessing over the bread and the wine, "This is my body, broken for you." The new covenant is one of humility and self-sacrifice so great that it even goes so far as to sacrifice one's own life. Peter claims he is ready and willing to make that kind of sacrifice for Jesus (Luke 22:33). But, as we know, he doesn't follow through on that promise. Yet.

Eventually, Peter did die for Jesus, but not that night. None of the disciples were capable of this kind of self-sacrificing love until they were given the Holy Spirit at Pentecost, when the new covenant really began. When Jeremiah and Ezekiel prophesied about the new covenant, God said it would involve a change of heart, being renewed from the inside (Jeremiah 31:31–34). God would put His Spirit in them. He would remove their hearts of stone and put in them hearts of flesh (Ezekiel 36:26–27). The only way His disciples could truly love the way Jesus loved was by having His Spirit living in them and loving through them.

QUESTIONS FOR REFLECTION

1. How would you describe someone who is selfless? Think of examples of people you know.

2. Why is it difficult to love this way? What do you have to give up in order to love like Jesus?

3. What does it mean to put the needs of others above your own? What are some specific ways you can do that with your friends, family, coworkers, neighbors, church, and community?

4. Where does God need to change your heart to help you love more like He does?

AS I HAVE LOVED YOU

The love of the new covenant is such a radical kind of love that the New Testament developed a whole new word to explain it, *agape*. The word *agape* is only used once outside of the Bible. It existed in Greek culture, but the New Testament adopted the term and filled it with rich meaning it didn't have before.

Agape is other-centered love. The sacrifice of self in the service of another. Though there are at least four words for love in Greek, only two of them appear in Scripture—*agape* and *phileo*. *Phileo* is the natural love people have for family and friends. *Agape* is the kind of love you choose to have for others, even if you don't have a natural *phileo* love for them.

In Scripture, *agape* is specifically used of the love of God (whom you could never repay) and love of the poor (who could never repay you). So when it's used of a human relationship—whether marriage, friendship, coworkers, or any other relationship—no element of repayment should enter in. A godly husband does good things for his wife without expecting anything in return. A godly friend forgives a friend who has hurt her; she doesn't hurt him in return. *Agape* love serves others, respects others, is kind to others even if they don't deserve it. Because none of us deserve the *agape* love of Jesus, and yet He gives it freely. As Jesus loves us, so we should love one another.

This is a divine kind of love because it cannot be found naturally in humanity. It comes only from God. There is no evolutionary, scientific reason for selfless *agape* love. It doesn't help the fittest survive. A humanistic worldview cannot lead to a truly altruistic, other-centered kind of love. As Jesus told His disciples, all human beings naturally love those who love them, but loving your enemy is something that comes only from God (Matthew 5:43–48). *Agape* is not an impulse generated by feelings; it's a choice. When God commands us to love our enemies, He's not telling us to have a good feeling toward them. He is telling us to *choose* to *act* in love, whether we feel like it or not.

This is what it means to be a follower of Christ. Paul tells us that we can do all the right things, but without the self-sacrificing love of Jesus it means nothing (1 Corinthians 13:1–3). Agape is essential to who we are and what we do as believers. When people see *agape* love in our lives, in our homes, and in our churches, they see a love that's not of this world.

QUESTIONS FOR REFLECTION

1. Who in your life is difficult for you to love? How is God calling you to reach out to them in love?

2. How is God calling you to love your enemies? What kind of an impact would it make on them if you were to show them real, true *agape* love?

3. What specific things can believers start doing to show *agape love to others, even to those who oppose us?*

4. What would it look like for you to live your life in an others-centered way? How would it change your priorities, your choices, your daily life?

BY THIS THEY WILL KNOW

This is the legacy Jesus left behind, the example of His Love. The kind of love that regards others as more important than ourselves (Philippians 2:3). The kind of love that doesn't insist on its own way (1 Corinthians 13:5). The kind of love that brings unity in diversity (Colossians 3:14). This is the heart of the gospel and what it means to be a Christian.

To be a disciple of Christ is to live as He lived. When we live like Him, love like Him, and serve like Him, it sends a message to those around us. They will see something different at work in us, a different kind of love. And many will be attracted to this kind of love, because we all want to be loved like that. We want to experience the kind of love that's willing to sacrifice—even to die—for another. May we be known for our love—in our families, our neighborhoods, our schools, our workplaces, our cities, and throughout the world. May people look at us and get a glimpse of the humility and self-sacrificing love of Jesus. May it cause them to say, "I want that kind of love."

QUESTIONS FOR REFLECTION

1. What message does it send to others when we, as believers, fail to love as He loved?

2. Why does Jesus tell us that the way we love one another will let others know we are His disciples (see John 13:35)?

3. When people look at your life, your family, your church community, in what ways can they see the radical, selfless love of Christ?

4. Who needs your love the most right now? How can you express that love to them? In what specific ways can you act in love toward them, even if you don't feel like it?

"NEVERTHELESS, I TELL YOU THE TRUTH:

IT IS TO YOUR ADVANTAGE THAT I GO

AWAY, FOR IF I DO NOT GO AWAY, THE

HELPER WILL NOT COME TO YOU. BUT IF I

GO, I WILL SEND HIM TO YOU."

—

JOHN 14-7

IT IS GOOD
THAT I GO

READ JOHN 14:1–31

THE FINAL DISCOURSE

We learned in the last lesson that meals were common settings in which rabbis taught their disciples. But this meal was especially significant. It was Passover, one of the three main festivals in Jewish culture, and Jesus knew it would be His last night with them before His death. These were His last words to His beloved disciples, what He wanted them to remember and live out after He was gone. It is the longest block of teaching in in the book of John, covering four entire chapters.

When we look at this discourse as a whole, we see one main purpose of Christ's teaching that night. Jesus is preparing them for the time when He will no longer be with them. Everything He said fit into that purpose. When He told them He would prepare a place for them in His Father's house. When He told them He is the way. When He told them the Father would send the Spirit to be with them. When He told them the world would hate them. When He told them He was the vine and they were the branches. This was His way of preparing them for when He was no longer with them in the flesh.

But the disciples were slow to understand. More than once, they misunderstood what He meant, and He had to explain further. Toward the end of His teaching, they literally said, "We do not know what He is talking about" (John 16:18). We may be tempted to be irritated with them, to think, *How could they not get it? They walked with Him for three years!* Even Jesus said to Philip, "Have I been with you so long, and you still do not know me, Philip?" But we have the advantage of hindsight. We know the end of the story.

At the time, Jesus's disciples really couldn't have imagined much of anything He was saying. They couldn't imagine that the Messiah would die, much less be resurrected. They still thought He would rule on a physical throne in Israel, and they would get to be His advisors (Mark 10:37). Though Peter had confessed that Jesus was the "Son of the living God," they couldn't really understand the concept of the Trinity yet.

Because Jesus was telling them what would happen when He was gone, these chapters deal extensively with the relationship and roles of the three persons of the Trinity. Jesus explained that He was going to the Father but that the Father would send the Holy Spirit to them instead. Jesus has existed with God forever and will exist forever, but His time on earth with them was coming to a close. Yet He reassured the disciples that even though He was going away, God would send His Spirit to be with them forever. God's Spirit would dwell in them and guide them in all truth. And, though they could never imagine it at the time, *that* was even better than having Jesus with them in the flesh.

THE ADVOCATE

Throughout this passage, Jesus primarily refers to the Holy Spirit as the Advocate or Helper. The word in Greek can mean intercessor, comforter, or advisor. The term has legal connotations, meaning a legal advocate or attorney. The Holy Spirit is our advocate. This Advocate is a supernatural Counselor, not merely a human one. He doesn't just give us legal advice; He actually *empowers* us to do the things Jesus commands.

Jesus called the Spirit "*another* Helper"—another of the same kind. The Spirit of God is not different from the Son of God in essence. Both are God. But He is different in form. He is Spirit, where the Son of God is God-made-flesh. Yet the Holy Spirit is not a force. He is a personal being, not an impersonal thing. Every pronoun referring to the Spirit in Scripture is "He," not "It," even though the word "spirit" would typically take a neuter pronoun. The Scriptures are intentional in showing us that the Spirit is a person, not a thing. The Westminster Confession of Faith states:

> In the unity of the Godhead there be three persons, of one substance, power, and eternity: God the Father, God the Son, and God the Holy Spirit: the Father is of none, neither begotten, nor proceeding; the Son is eternally begotten of the Father; the Holy Spirit eternally proceeding from the Father and the Son.[3]

---

[3] *The Westminster Confession of Faith* (The Presbyterian Church in America, 2007), 2.3.

Jesus reassured them that though He was leaving, He was not leaving them alone. "If anyone loves me, he will keep my word, and my Father will love him and we will come to him and make our home with him" (v. 23). We—Father, Son, and Holy Spirit—will *make our home* with him.

Throughout all of Scripture, the greatest promise God ever made to His people was that He would dwell with them. This was the entire goal in establishing the covenant with Israel. God told Israel, "I will take you to be my people. . . . I will bring you into the land. . . . I will dwell among [you] and be [your] God" (Exodus 6:7–8; 29:45). In the Old Testament, God dwelled among His people in the Holy of Holies, in the tabernacle, at the very center of their camp. All the other tents were around it. God lived among them, right in the middle of their mess.

In Jesus, God went a step further by sending His Son to dwell among us—God in human form. Jesus walked with them, talked with them, ate with them, cried with them—He made His home with them. He walked this earth as a human being, as one of us. The name "Immanuel" even means "God with us." He was God with skin on; God that people could see and touch. At the beginning of his Gospel, John wrote that when Jesus came down, He "pitched his tent" among us. Eugene Peterson paraphrased it in *The Message*, "The Word became flesh and blood and moved into the neighborhood."

Now, Jesus was promising that the Holy Spirit would do the same, but even more closely. The Spirit would come and make His home *in our* hearts. The Greek word for the Spirit means "one who is called to the side of another." The Spirit has been "called to our side" by the Father, sent to walk with us every day. Because Jesus was leaving His disciples, the Spirit was sent to walk with them instead. But the Holy Spirit is an even greater help than Jesus, because He didn't just walk next to them, He dwelled *inside them.*

This was such a game-changer for the relationship between God and humanity that the prophets said when this happened, it would be a whole new covenant. Jeremiah explicitly says the new covenant in Christ "will not be like the old covenant." Instead of just teaching them the Law, God would put the Law within them. He would write it on their hearts (Jeremiah 31:31–34). It would no longer be external. It would be inside them by the power of the Holy Spirit. The prophet Ezekiel says that God will take away their hearts of stone and give them a heart of flesh. "I will put My Spirit within you, and you shall live" (Ezekiel 37:14).

This was a new thing God was doing. Something changes in this new covenant. The Holy Spirit is the same yesterday, today, and forever, but the way He moved in people's lives was very different from the old to the new covenant. In the Old Testament, the Holy Spirit *came upon* someone for a task or a leadership role. And He left when that task was completed or if the person disobeyed. But the Spirit *dwelled* in the tabernacle behind the veil of the Holy of Holies, where only the high priest could enter once a year. When Jesus died, the veil was torn in two and the Holy Spirit was made available to all who would come. Today, we have unlimited access to the Holy Spirit. We don't have to go to a tabernacle or temple to meet with God. We are the temple. The Holy Spirit dwells inside us.

The Spirit is able to be our Helper in whole new way because He lives in us. The Holy Spirit doesn't just remind us of what Jesus taught, He teaches us Himself from the inside (John 14:26). Paul wrote that the Holy Spirit supernaturally imparts spiritual wisdom to us through spiritual means. He reveals to us things we could not understand by human wisdom or teaching, a secret and hidden wisdom of God only understood by those who have the Spirit (1 Corinthians 2:6–16). The Spirit doesn't just tell us what we should do or how we should live. He has the power to change us from the inside out. This is why Jeremiah and Ezekiel can say that with the Spirit now dwelling inside us, we will finally be able to keep the Law (Ezekiel 36:27). The Holy Spirit being our Advocate or Counselor isn't simply about giving us good advice. It's about making us new creations, giving us new hearts, growing His fruit within us, and changing us from the inside out.

QUESTIONS FOR REFLECTION

1. Recall a time when the Holy Spirit helped you in a situation or a decision. What did He do or say?

2. How is it that Holy Spirit enables us to keep the Law?

3. In what area of your life would you like to see the Holy Spirit change you?

READ JOHN 15:1–11 AND 26–27

THE VINE AND THE BRANCHES

Again, Jesus's teaching in this final discourse focuses on the three different persons of the Trinity and how they interact with humanity. He explicitly said that He is the vine, the Father is the vinedresser, and we are the branches. Yet, when we read this passage in context, we can also see an implication about the role of the Spirit. Overall, this discourse focuses on how the Spirit will work in the disciples' lives after Jesus was gone. Jesus returned to teaching about the Helper again and again at the end of each chapter, including this one.

In this metaphor, Jesus is the vine and if we abide in Him, if we *remain* in Him, we can bear much fruit. We are only branches. If we are cut off from the vine, we will shrivel up and die. But if we stay connected to the vine, we will receive nourishment and be able to bear fruit. In Galatians, Paul calls this "the fruit of the Spirit," the things the Holy Spirit grows in our hearts and lives as we walk with Him (Galatians 5:22–25). These are not different fruits, some from Jesus and some from the Spirit. They are two ways of talking about the same thing. The fruit of the Spirit is the fruit that comes from abiding in Jesus. The *way* we abide in Jesus is through the Holy Spirit. Jesus is the vine, but the Spirit is the *life* that comes through the vine into the branches to bear fruit. The Father sends the Spirit to abide in us. That is how we abide in Christ.

The only way we can "walk by the Spirit" is by abiding in Christ (Galatians 5:22–25). Apart from Christ, we can do nothing (John 15:5). And we can only abide in Christ because the Spirit dwells in us (1 Corinthians 3:16). The New Testament uses two interchangeable phrases to describe union with Christ:

→ We are in Christ (John 15:1–7; 2 Corinthians 5:17; 12:2; Galatians 3:28; Ephesians 1:3–4; 2:10; Philippians 3:9; 1 Thessalonians 4:16; 1 John 4:13)
→ Christ is in us (Romans 8:10; 2 Corinthians 13:5; Galatians 2:20; Ephesians 3:17; Colossians 1:27)

Three other passages combine *both* of these concepts (John 6:56; 15:4; 1 John 4:13). We are in Christ and Christ is in us through the Holy Spirit, the Helper the Father sends (John 15:26).

Our salvation is not in our own strength but in the work of Christ (Ephesians 2:8–10). It is the same with our sanctification. Our Christian life isn't about trying harder to do better to follow God's Law. It is about union with Christ. We don't seek to do better; we seek Christ. We don't simply work harder to be more patient or more loving or more peaceful. Those are fruits the Spirit grows in us over time. Just as it takes months for a seed to grow into a flower and years for a garden to grow into maturity, it takes months and years for the fruit of the Spirit to blossom in our lives. As we walk with the Spirit (Galatians 5:16), as we set our minds on things above (Colossians 3:2), as we seek Christ's kingdom and His righteousness (Matthew 6:33), as we stay connected to the vine (John 15:1–11). Apart from Him, we can do nothing.

Just as we could not save ourselves, we cannot live a godly life ourselves. We were dead in our trespasses and sins (Ephesians 2:1). But God made us alive in Christ (Ephesians 2:5). He made us new creations in Christ, "God's workmanship," created in Christ for good works (Ephesians 2:10). In the Greek, that word *workmanship* means "work of art." We are His handiwork, His work of art, *created to do good works*. Because God has made us alive in Christ, we can do good works. Because God has united us with Christ, we can bear much fruit (John 15:5). God is the source of life. The only reason we can live the life God has called us to live is that Christ lives in us. We cannot do good apart from Him.

The Christian life is not a self-help, try-harder, do-better religion. It is a daily reality of abiding in Christ. It is choosing every day to die to self, to take up our cross, and to follow Jesus. Wherever He leads. To help us do that, God sent His Spirit to dwell with us and in us. To keep us connected to the vine and to bear His fruit in us. Because of the Holy Spirit, even though Christ was leaving them physically, the disciples could *remain* with Him spiritually.

The Greek word translated "abide" here means to remain, to stay, or to continue. Jesus says in 15:16 that he "chose" and "appointed" us to bear fruit. So, even when our devotion is lukewarm or sporadic, our confidence is in the God who is at work in us to bear the fruit he determined for us. Through the Spirit, we abide in Jesus, remain in Jesus, stay connected to Jesus. We need to be constantly connected to the source—the vine—to receive strength and sustenance and bear fruit. And that is why He sent His Spirit—so we could stay connected to Him.

QUESTIONS FOR REFLECTION

1. Does abiding in Christ mean we have to pray all day long or live as monks with nothing worldly in our lives at all? If not, what does it mean?

2. Read Ephesians 5:22-23. Which of the qualities of the fruit of the Spirit are strong in you? Which ones need more growth?

3. Name one way in which the Spirit has helped you grow and mature this past year.

4. In what ways would you like to be more fruitful in your life?

READ JOHN 16:4-15

HE WILL CONVICT THE WORLD

In these passages, Jesus taught His disciples a lot about the Holy Spirit. The Spirit helps us, advocates for us, and comforts us. He is the Spirit of truth. He teaches us all things and reminds us of what Jesus taught. The world cannot accept Him because it doesn't see Him or know Him. But we know Him because He lives in us, and He will be with us forever.

Other passages say the Spirit prays for us when we don't know how to pray (Romans 8:26). He guided the disciples and told them where to go and what to do (Acts 8:39 and *many* others). He strengthens us and gives us power (Acts 1:8; Ephesians 3:16-19). He brings freedom and joy (2 Corinthians 3:17; 1 Thessalonians 1:6). He speaks prophecy through us and reveals things to us (1 Corinthians 2:10; 2 Peter 1:21). He bears fruit in us and gives us spiritual gifts (Galatians 5; 1 Corinthians 12). He washes us, renews us, sanctifies us, and transforms us (2 Corinthians 3:18; 2 Thessalonians 2:13; Titus 3:5). He puts the flesh to death, gives us life, seals us, and lives in us (Romans 8:11-13; 1 Corinthians 3:16; Ephesians 1:13).

In this passage in particular, Jesus added that the Spirit convicts *the world* concerning sin, righteousness, and judgment. He specifies exactly why the Holy Spirit is the One who convicts the world—because they do not believe in Him, because Jesus was going to the Father, and because the ruler of the world had been judged. Because the world is the object of the conviction, all three of these points are about the Holy Spirit convicting the world, not believers. The "because" in each phrase indicates that this is telling us *why* the Spirit is convicting the world.

Because they don't believe in Jesus, the Spirit convicts the world of their sin. He shows them why they need Jesus. Because the ruler of this world has been judged and defeated on the cross, now it is time for the Spirit to come in a new way. The Holy Spirit was not sent only for the disciples. He also came for the world—to convict them of their sin, to call them to repent and trust in Jesus. The Holy Spirit speaks directly to the heart on a spiritual level. We can preach and teach God's word, present logical apologetic arguments, and share testimonies of how God changed our lives, but we can't convict someone's heart. Only God can do that (1 Corinthians 3:1-9). Though we can and should tell people about Jesus every day, the Spirit is the One who convicts them of their sin, calls them to repent, and changes their hearts.

QUESTIONS FOR REFLECTION

1. If it is the Spirit who convicts of sin and changes people's hearts, then what role can we play in leading people to Jesus?

2. How does knowing the Spirit is the One who convicts people about their sin, how does that affect the way we pray for them? The way we witness to them?

3. Make a list of the people you know who don't yet know Jesus. Pray for each one by name and ask God to give you love and courage to witness to them.

IT IS TO YOUR ADVANTAGE

Knowing all that the Holy Spirit would do in their lives, Jesus told the disciples that it was to their advantage for Him to go away so the Holy Spirit could come to them. Jesus commissioned them not only to carry on His ministry but to take it even further—to the ends of the earth (Matthew 28:18–20; Acts 1:8), which is something they couldn't have done without the power of the Holy Spirit. The Spirit completely revolutionized their ministry.

At the beginning of the book of Acts, after Jesus had been resurrected, appeared to them for forty days, and was about to ascend into heaven, He told them to wait in Jerusalem for the baptism of the Holy Spirit (Acts 1:1–4). Jesus said, "You will receive power when the Holy Spirit has come upon you, and you will be My witnesses in Jerusalem and in all Judea and Samaria, and to the end of the earth" (Acts 1:8). The purpose of the power of the Holy Spirit was to enable them to be His witnesses.

The Spirit gave them the *understanding* to preach the gospel. The last time we saw the disciples, before Pentecost, they still thought the kingdom was about restoring Israel. Even though they had seen Jesus resurrected and He had been with them for forty days, teaching them more and more, they still didn't seem to get it theologically. But after Pentecost, they preached the gospel with a supernatural understanding of the Scriptures and their fulfillment in Christ (Acts 2; 7). It was the Holy Spirit who made the difference.

The Spirit gave them the *boldness* to preach the gospel. A few hours after this Upper Room Discourse on the night of Jesus's death, all but one of the disciples fled from Jesus in fear of the Jewish leaders who wanted to kill Him. Peter denied even knowing Jesus. Only John was left at the foot of the cross. In their own strength, there was no way they would have had the boldness to preach the gospel to a hostile world. But after they received the power of the Holy Spirit at Pentecost, Peter and John preached boldly right in front of the same rulers, elders, and scribes who plotted to kill Jesus (Acts 4:1–12). And when those leaders warned them not to preach the gospel anymore, they went back to the church community and prayed for boldness to preach without fear, no matter what threat there was against them. And God filled them with the Spirit so that they continued to preach boldly, even though their lives were in danger (Acts 4:23–31). It was the Holy Spirit who made the difference.

The Spirit also gave them the power to do supernatural signs and wonders to support their message (e.g., Acts 5:12; 8:13), not as a parlor tricks or for their own fame and glory, but so people would believe the disciples were from God and that their message was true. All the supernatural power the Holy Spirit gave the disciples was about one thing—being witnesses for Jesus to the ends of the earth. As Jesus taught in this discourse, the Spirit would glorify Christ (John 16:14). The Helper would teach them all things and bring to their remembrance all that Jesus had taught them (John 14:26). The Helper would bear witness about Jesus, and the disciples would also bear witness (John 15:26–27). Because of the Holy Spirit, the disciples would have the power, boldness, and understanding to be His witnesses to the world.

Our mission is the same as the disciples' mission. We are called to be His witnesses to the world. We know that only the Spirit convicts people's hearts, but as witnesses we are called to testify about what Christ has done in our lives. The Holy Spirit was not only sent to us to grow fruit in our lives, but also to empower us to share the gospel with others. This is our role in God's redemptive story. We can't control whether others accept Christ, but it is our responsibility to share the good news. As Paul wrote, how will people hear and believe unless someone shares the good news with them (Romans 10:14–17)?

QUESTIONS FOR REFLECTION

1. Do you ever have fears or doubts about being a witness? If so, what are they?

2. How does it encourage you that the Holy Spirit can empower you to be a witness for Christ?

3. Describe someone you know who is bold in sharing the good news of Jesus with others. What are they like?

AND SHE SAW TWO ANGELS IN WHITE,

SITTING WHERE THE BODY OF JESUS

HAD LAIN, ONE AT THE HEAD AND ONE

AT THE FEET. THEY SAID TO HER,

"WOMAN, WHY ARE YOU WEEPING?"

—

JOHN 20:12-13A

CRUCIFIXION
AND RESURRECTION

READ JOHN 18:1-11

THE ARREST

After His final teaching, Jesus prayed for His disciples in the Upper Room. He prayed for God to protect them from the evil one, sanctify them in the truth, and unify them as He and the Father are unified. These are things the Holy Spirit would do for them when Jesus was gone, things they would need in order to be effective in their mission. Just as Jesus had prepared them through His teaching, He also prepared them through His prayers (John 17:6–19).

When Jesus finished praying, he led his disciples to the garden of Gethsemane, where Matthew, Mark, and Luke record Jesus praying again, but John does not. In the versions of the other Gospels, Jesus goes off alone and prays for an hour, returning to find the disciples asleep. This happens three times, and each time, Jesus chastises them for not being able to stay awake and keep watch. Those prayers were each an hour long, but the only thing the Gospel writers recorded was Jesus asking the Lord to remove the cup of suffering from Him, if it be God's will. But if not, Jesus said, "Your will be done" (Matthew 26:42).

John does not record those prayers, but that doesn't mean they didn't happen or that John forgot about them. He simply didn't focus on that part of the story. John wrote his Gospel much later than the other three, and his readers would have been familiar with them. He wanted to tell the story in a different way. Though John does not record this prayer, he does portray the same resolve in Jesus. Throughout this passage, John paints a picture of a Jesus who knew His mission and was fully committed to follow through with it.

Judas left the Passover meal after the footwashing, but before any of Jesus's final teaching (John 13:18–30). But John tells us that the garden of Gethsemane was a regular meeting place for Jesus and His disciples, so it was a natural place for Judas to find Him if the group was no longer in the Upper Room. Jesus predicted that Judas would be the one to betray Him by quoting a psalm, "Even my close friend in whom I trusted, who ate my bread, has lifted his heel against me" (Psalm 41:9). Jesus explicitly told them that He predicted Judas's betrayal so that when it happened, "You may believe that I am he" (John 13:19).

The NIV says, "So that you will believe that I am who I am." Throughout Scripture, when talking about the purpose of miracles and prophesies, God often repeats the phrase, "then you will know that I am God" (e.g., Exodus 6:7; 1 Kings 20:13; Ezekiel 20:44). Miracles and prophecies aren't tricks or shows. They are signs used to give power to God's message—so people would believe that Yahweh was God, listen to His message, repent, and turn back to Him. The same is true for Jesus. His signs and wonders were performed so people would believe He was from God (John 14:11).

But that phrase, "You will believe that I am who I am," means more than simply that Jesus was *from* God. It means that He was God. This is the exact phrase God used at the burning bush when He told Moses His personal name, Yahweh—"I Am." God said to Moses, "I am who I am" (Exodus 3:14). Throughout the book of John, Jesus claimed He was God with each of His "I Am" statements. When He said "I am the good shepherd" or "I am the living water," He was claiming to be the "Great I Am." Jesus even made the bold statement, "Before Abraham was, I am," after which the people tried to stone Him for blasphemy because they knew that in this statement He was claiming to be God Himself (John 8:58).

In the other Gospels' versions of the story, Judas signaled to the soldiers which one was Jesus with a kiss. But in John's version, when Judas arrived with the soldiers, Jesus simply asked them who they were looking for. When they said, "Jesus of Nazareth," Jesus answered, "I am he." But this wasn't just a simple "Oh, that's me" response. It was deeply theological, connected to every other "I Am" statement Jesus made in John's Gospel.

And Jesus's response had a supernatural effect. When Jesus said, "I am he," all of the soldiers, chief priests, and Pharisees drew back and fell to the ground. His enemies—the ones who had come to arrest Him and have Him killed—fell at His feet. This was not an act of worship. They didn't change their minds and follow Jesus. They were arresting Him for claiming to be king of the Jews, and here in this moment, God showed them who Jesus really is—the "Great I Am." Jesus is the King of kings and Lord of lords; and one day, every knee will bow in heaven and on earth and under the earth, whether they want to or not, even His enemies (Philippians 2:9–11).

Jesus could have fought to save Himself. But He wasn't there to fight a physical battle. He was there to fight a spiritual one. Not with swords and spears, but by giving His life. As Isaiah prophesied, Jesus was the Suffering Servant who went willingly to His death (Isaiah 53:7–9). Though He was God, He humbled Himself and became obedient to death, even death on a cross (Philippians 2:8).

QUESTIONS FOR REFLECTION

1. What does it say about Jesus and His mission that He went to the cross willingly?

2. What does Jesus's reaction teach you about obedience to God?

3. In what ways are humility and obedience related?

READ JOHN 18:12–19:16

THE TRIAL

It was a long night for Jesus. He had been awake all day, and then had prayed intensely for three hours in the garden while the disciples slept. His soul was so distraught during that prayer time that "His sweat became like great drops of blood falling down to the ground" (Luke 22:44). He was already exhausted before He was even arrested. Then He was questioned by several different leaders, both religious and secular. Because the Jews were in a territory of the Roman Empire, they were not allowed to execute anyone. So Jesus was tried first before the religious court of the Jews and then before the Roman governor.

We can learn more detail about Jesus's trial by piecing together the story from all of the Gospels, but in every account, we see that His trial is suspiciously fast. The Sanhedrin broke their own laws with Jesus's trial in at least the following ways:

→ Capital trials had to meet during the day.
→ They were supposed to have advance notice so that as many members of the Sanhedrin could be there as possible. At least half was required for a quorum.
→ Their meeting was held in a private home rather than their official chambers in the temple.
→ They could render a verdict only after an entire day and night had passed.
→ Trials were forbidden on the Sabbath and during festivals.

→ Executions were forbidden during a festival, with rare exceptions for the most heinous crimes.

→ They were supposed to diligently cross-examine witnesses; and if they contradicted one another, their testimony was thrown out and the false witnesses executed.

→ Interrogators were not supposed to try to force the accused to convict himself.

→ Though a public flogging was not illegal, splitting at, striking, and taunting Him were against Jewish law.

The priestly aristocracy was in a hurry. They were afraid that if they waited until morning, more supporters of Jesus would arise in the crowd. So, they did a quick "trial" of their own and then pressured the Roman governor to crucify Jesus that very night. John doesn't record the trial before the Sanhedrin or even the questioning before the high priest. He records only Jesus's refusal to answer their questions, continuing to show Him as willingly going to His death, "like a lamb that is led to the slaughter" (Isaiah 53:7).

John's account of the interrogations of Jesus is much briefer than the other Gospels. The other Gospels show more detail and more back-and-forth between the Sanhedrin, the high priest, Herod, and Pilate. By keeping his account simple, John focused more on the theological point he wanted to make, the same point he made with Peter's actions in the garden. That Jesus, the Son of God, allowed Himself to be sacrificed as the new covenant Passover Lamb.

When the religious leaders presented Jesus before Pilate, they had a different accusation—that Jesus claimed to be king of the Jews. This claim would have been a threat to Roman rule, something they thought would convince Pilate to convict Him. But Jesus surprised Pilate by answering that He had no desire to fight for the throne, because His kingdom is not from this world (18:36). When Pilate warns Jesus that he had authority over Jesus's life and death, Jesus told Pilate he had that authority only because God gave it to him (19:11). Jesus refused to answer their accusations, even though He knew it would lead to His death. He refused to fight, even though He could have called down legions of angels to save Him. Again, John is showing us that Jesus willingly offered Himself as a sacrifice.

Pilate wanted to release Jesus. He tried several times and in several ways. Even as he took his place on the judgment seat, Pilate never declared Jesus guilty. In fact, he continued to call Jesus their king, declaring, "Behold your King" (19:14), then asking, "Shall I crucify your King?" And then, on the sign over Jesus's head, he wrote, "the King of the Jews" (19:20). When the chief priests asked him to change it, Pilate refused. He did not believe Jesus was guilty, but the pressure from the Jews was too great, and he finally let them have what they wanted.

John paints a picture of a complete sham of a trial, rigged from the start with Pilate as a pawn to get the death penalty for Jesus. Jesus even said the high priest was more responsible than Pilate (v. 11). Pilate himself emphasized the sham of the trial when he answered Jesus with, "What is truth?" The whole trial made a mockery of truth. The men accusing Jesus didn't care about truth. They cared about power. This trial was proof that in this world, whoever was in power determined whatever "truth" they wanted. But Jesus, King of another world, is *the* Truth. Jesus's exchange with Pilate serves to remind us of what John emphasized from the very beginning of his gospel—that Jesus came to bring light to a dark world, but the people would not accept Him because they loved the darkness (John 1:10; 3:19).

John tells us it was the day of preparation of the Passover. The chief priests should have been preparing the people's sacrifices for the Passover meal. Instead, they were preparing for the sacrifice of the new covenant Passover Lamb. Pilate handed Jesus over to them, and it was they who took Jesus out to the place of the crucifixion. The same chief priests who refused to enter Pilate's house so they would not be defiled for the Passover meal had no problem framing and executing on Passover an innocent man they saw as a threat to their power. This is the very definition of the empty, worthless religion God said in the Prophets that He hated (e.g., Isaiah 58; Amos 5). The chief priests proved themselves to be exactly what Jesus had said they were during His ministry—power-hungry hypocrites.

QUESTIONS FOR REFLECTION

1. Why is it significant that Jesus was innocent? How does that make His sacrifice for our sin effective?

2. Why was Jesus a threat to the religious leaders?

3. How does sin make us blind to the truth?

READ JOHN 19:16–42

THE CRUCIFIXION

Pilate handed Jesus over to the chief priests, who walked him to the crucifixion. Because it was the day of preparation, the priests would have been slaughtering lambs for the Passover all day long. So, Jesus, the new covenant Passover Lamb was crucified at the same time that the old covenant Passover lambs were being slaughtered in the temple. John emphasized this connection between the old covenant and the new covenant in his telling of Jesus's death. In His crucifixion, Jesus fulfilled a number of Old Testament Scriptures, some of which John explicitly said were being fulfilled:

- → The soldiers cast lots for his clothes (v. 24; Psalm 22:18).
- → They gave him sour wine to drink (v. 28; Psalm 69:21).
- → None of His bones were broken (v. 36; Psalm 34:20).
- → They looked on the One they had pierced (v. 20; Psalm 22:17; Zechariah 12:10).
- → There were others that John didn't mention:
- → He was sold for thirty pieces of silver (Zechariah 11:12).
- → He was oppressed yet didn't open his mouth (Isaiah 53:7).
- → They mocked Him (Psalm 22:7-8).
- → They spit on Him and shamed Him (Isaiah 50:6).
- → His body was scourged (Isaiah 52:14).
- → He was brought like a lamb to the slaughter (Isaiah 53:7).
- → He was counted among sinners (Isaiah 53:12).
- → His hands and feet were pierced (Psalm 22:16).
- → They mockingly asked why God didn't deliver Him (Psalm 22:8).
- → He prayed for those who killed Him (Isaiah 53:12).
- → He committed His Spirit into God's hands (Psalm 31:5).

All these things point to the Old Testament prophecies being fulfilled, the same testimony John the Baptist declared in the first chapter of John's Gospel. Jesus is the Messiah, the Lamb of God who takes away the sins of the world (John 1:29). John's sole purpose in writing his Gospel was so his readers would believe that Jesus is the Christ, the Son of God, and that believing, they may have life in His name (John 20:31). In John's account of the crucifixion, every sign points to this truth. Every detail is intentionally written as evidence to support his case.

QUESTIONS FOR REFLECTION

1. How does Jesus's fulfillment of Old Testament prophesies strengthen John's case?

2. How was Jesus's sacrifice a once-for-all offering for sin (see Hebrews 10)?

3. What does Jesus's death on the cross say about God's love? What does it say about His justice?

READ JOHN 20

THE RESURRECTION

The resurrection is the climax of John's story, what he has been building up to. His Gospel opens with the statement, "In Him was life, and the life was the light of men" (1:14) and closes with his objective, "That you may have life in His name" (20:31). As we saw in our very first lesson, the Gospel of John reiterates this purpose—eternal life—over and over throughout its entirety. The resurrection shows us how this will happen.

Each Gospel's account of the resurrection is slightly different, but that doesn't mean they conflict. In any eyewitness testimony, we expect some details to be remembered differently. If the stories of multiple witnesses are identical, then authorities typically believe they are fabricated. It is only natural to see slight differences in each account. In every version, a group of women went to the tomb early in the morning on the first day of the week to anoint the body with spices. In every story, they saw an empty tomb and an angel. The Gospels differ regarding whether the stone was already rolled away or the women saw it being rolled away, whether there was one angel or two, and whether the angels were inside the tomb or sitting on the stone. The details are slightly different, but the main points are the same.

John's telling of the story is unique in that it features the "beloved disciple," John himself, outrunning Peter to the tomb, and it shows an intimate moment between Jesus and Mary Magdalene. Just as a woman was the first person to whom He revealed His identity as the Messiah, a woman was the first person to whom He appeared after His death. When He appeared to Mary, she did not recognize Him. She thought He was the gardener. But when He spoke her name, she immediately knew who He was. This is consistent with John's very personal narrative, showing Jesus as a real person with a deep love for His people, a close friend of John, Peter, Mary, and the other disciples.

Before Jesus revealed Himself to Mary, she had seen only an empty tomb and ran to tell the disciples. She didn't think that He had been resurrected. She thought someone had moved the body. Peter and John ran to the tomb after hearing Mary's testimony. They didn't stroll. They didn't even walk quickly. The Greek says they ran like an athlete running to the finish line. John doesn't record Peter's reaction when he saw the empty tomb, but when John saw it, the text simply says, "He saw and believed." John tells us that up to this point they didn't understand the Scriptures, that Jesus must rise from the dead (v. 9). But as soon as John saw the empty tomb, he believed.

The resurrection is the key to our entire faith. Paul wrote that if Jesus was not resurrected, then our entire faith is meaningless (1 Corinthians 15:14). Without the resurrection, the cross means nothing. Without Easter Sunday, Good Friday isn't good. It's tragic. The resurrection is the linchpin to the entire apologetic argument of Christianity. Christ's sacrificial work was done on the cross. But the Resurrection proved His triumph over death.

Resurrection is the opposite of death, the reversal of death. It is *eternal* life. When Jesus was resurrected, it reversed death not just for Himself, but for all who believe in Him (Romans 6:4–5). Jesus's resurrection means we will one day be resurrected too, in glorified bodies that will not perish (1 Corinthians 15:42). It's not just human beings who will be affected. All of creation will be made new, a new heaven and a new earth (Revelation 21).

The resurrection changes everything. It changes what our faith is even about. Before the Resurrection, people thought of Jesus as a great moral teacher. His disciples thought He was the Messiah, even the Son of God. As disciples, their role was to follow their Rabbi, to live the way He taught and modeled for them. In the Jewish faith, following a Rabbi is really just about learning how to follow the law better. Even today, that's what some people think Christianity is all about—morality rather than the true gospel.

And this is where the resurrection makes all the difference. If Jesus were still in the tomb, we could think of Him as a good teacher or a moral example to follow. But if He is alive, then He is so much more than a great moral teacher. He is God. And our faith is about so much more than trying to be a good person. It's about God making dead people alive (Ephesians 2:5).

In Christ, we don't become better versions of ourselves. We go from being dead to being alive. It's a completely different concept. When Paul explained it in Ephesians 2, he opened with "You were dead in your sins." Dead people can't make moral choices. The gospel isn't about us doing better at following Jesus; it's about God making us a new creation so we can live like Him. Like the dry bones in Ezekiel's vision, God breathes His Spirit in us to make us alive (Ezekiel 37:1–6). God can make alive what is dead. That is the good news of the resurrection.

QUESTIONS FOR REFLECTION

1. In what ways does the resurrection give you hope today?

2. What does it mean that we have no hope if Jesus was not raised from the dead?

3. How would you respond to someone who says, "I've tried to be a good person, and I think that's what matters to God"?

4. What place does morality have in the life of a Christian?

5. How does the gospel differ from other major religions, which depend on good works to earn salvation?

AND THE SOLDIERS TWISTED TOGETHER

A CROWN OF THORNS AND PUT IT ON HIS

HEAD AND ARRAYED HIM IN A PURPLE

ROBE. THEY CAME UP TO HIM, SAYING,

"HAIL, KING OF THE JEWS!"

AND STRUCK HIM WITH THEIR HANDS.

—

JOHN 19:2-3

PROPHET,
PRIEST,
and KING

JOHN 1, 2, 6, 10, 12, 17, 19

READ JOHN 7:10–12 AND 40–44

MIXED REACTIONS

Throughout the book of John, people had many different reactions to Jesus. In chapter 7 alone, some said He was "a good man" and others that He was leading people astray. Some said He really was the prophet, while others believed He was the Messiah. But then others said He couldn't be, because He came from Galilee. People said He must be the Messiah because He had performed so many miracles, but some thought He was possessed by a demon. Some didn't know who He was, but they were amazed at His teaching. Some wanted to defend Him, and some wanted to kill Him.

On one end of the spectrum were people who believed He was the Messiah, the Savior of Israel. On the other were people who opposed Him and wanted Him dead. Those in between were doubting or uncertain.

Some things about Jesus seemed to indicate He was the Messiah they had been promised—His miracles and His teaching had to have come from God. But they expected the Messiah, the son of David, to be a conquering hero who would overthrow Rome and establish Israel as an independent nation again, as in David's day. They expected a military leader like the judges of old and a powerful king like David.

In Matthew, Jesus asked His disciples, "Who do people say that I am?" They answered, "Some say John the Baptist, others say Elijah, and others Jeremiah or one of the prophets" (Matthew 16:14). Then Jesus asked, "But who do you say that I am?" He wanted to know what His closest followers believed about Him. It's as if Jesus were saying, "The world may not understand who I am, but do you?" Peter answered, "You are the Christ, the son of the living God!" Peter doesn't say, "You are the Christ, the conquering hero who will restore the kingdom to Israel." He says, "... the Christ, the son of the living God." Peter confessed something similar in John 6, when He said, "Lord, to whom shall we go? You have words of eternal life, and we have believed, and have come to know, that You are the Holy One of God" (John 6:68–69). Peter not only believed Jesus is Messiah, but he also understood who Messiah really is.

Today, if Jesus were to ask "Who do you say that I am?" people might have a lot of different responses:

- → He's my buddy.
- → He's a great moral teacher, a religious leader, but that's it.
- → Jesus was a social transformer, rebel, and activist.
- → Jesus is one of many ways to heaven, just like Buddha or Mohammad, etc.
- → And on and on and on...

Many people are willing to accept Jesus as a great moral teacher or example, but to say He is the Son of God is another story. To believe that faith in Him is the only way to be saved is just too much for many in our culture to believe.

People in Jesus's day thought the same thing. That's why people so often tried to stone Him for blasphemy and the high priest tried to have Him sentenced to death (e.g., Matthew 26:65; John 10:31). The Jews of Jesus's day thought the Messiah would be a messenger from God, the anointed of God, a prophet of God, but never God Himself.

And yet, that's exactly who Jesus claimed to be. Throughout His ministry, with every "I Am" statement, Jesus was claiming to be God, the "Great I Am" Himself. He explicitly said, "I and the Father are one" (John 10:30), and "If you had known Me, you would know My Father also. From now on you do know Him and have seen Him" (John 14:7). As C. S. Lewis argued in *Mere Christianity*, you really can't say Jesus was a good moral teacher when He claimed to be God. There are really only two choices. Either He actually was God or He was a blasphemer who deserved the death penalty. There is no middle ground. Lewis wrote,

> A man who said the sort of things Jesus said would not be a great moral teacher. He would either be a lunatic—on a level with a man who says he is a poached egg—or else He would be the Devil of Hell. You must make your choice. Either this man was, and is, the Son of God; or else a madman or something worse. You can shut Him up for a fool, you can spit at Him and kill Him as a demon; or you can fall at His feet

and call Him Lord and God. But let us not come with any patronizing nonsense about His being a great human teacher. He has not left that open to us. He did not intend to.[4]

WHO IS THE MESSIAH?

Jesus claimed to be the Messiah, but the Messiah was so much more than what people expected. They expected a human king sent from God. But Jesus claimed to be a divine king—God Himself. This is what He meant when He told Pilate that His kingdom is not of this world. That's why Jesus's favorite title for Himself was not Messiah or even Son of God. It was Son of Man (e.g., Mark 10:45). When the high priest said, "Tell us if You are the Messiah, the Son of God," Jesus answered that He was the Son of Man (Matthew 26:62–64).

If we just heard the phrase "Son of Man" but didn't study its usage in the Bible, it would be logical to think "Son of Man" refers to Jesus's humanity and "Son of God" refers to His divinity. Actually, both phrases refer to Jesus's divinity. The term "Son of Man" comes from a vision of the heavenly throne in Daniel 7. In his vision, Daniel saw four great beasts, which represented four kingdoms of the world. The beasts boasted before the throne of God, whom Daniel described as "the Ancient of Days." Then, "one like a son of man" came before the throne, and the Ancient of Days gave Him all authority, glory, and sovereign power and all of the people of every nation, tribe, and tongue worshiped Him" (Daniel 7:1–14). Reading this passage now, it seems clear that the Messianic king *is* the Son of Man to whom all authority, honor, and power will be given forever. But to the Jews of Jesus's time, the Messiah would be a human king sent from God, while the Son of Man was a divine being.

But Jesus combined these two images to say that He is both the Messianic king and the Son of Man from Daniel 7. The Messiah is the Son of Man. Jesus used this title as a way to explain to the people that the Messiah was more than they had expected. The Messiah was not just a human king of the line of David who would bring Israel back to its former glory. The Messiah is a divine figure who will reign forever on the throne of heaven. The kingdom of God is not a physical nation but a spiritual kingdom that transcends every nation.

So when Jesus is asked by the high priest if He is the Messiah, the Son of God, and He answers by talking about the Son of Man, it makes sense that the high priests responded by accusing Him of blasphemy. Jesus was claiming to be not just the Messiah, a human king sent from God. He was claiming to be a divine king—God Himself.

QUESTIONS FOR REFLECTION

1. If someone were to say to you, "I think Jesus was a good moral teacher, just like Mohammad or Buddha or Gandhi, but that's it," how would you respond?

2. How does viewing Jesus as a King with authority over your life different than seeing Him as a great moral teacher?

---

[4] C. S. Lewis, *Mere Christianity* (NY: Macmillan / Collier, 1952), 55.

PROPHET, PRIEST, AND KING

The people expected the Messiah to be a conquering king, a son of David who would overthrow Rome, reestablish Israel as its own nation, and bring back its former glory. But the Messiah is so much more. In Israel's theocracy, there were three distinct anointed leadership roles—prophet, priest, and king.

A prophet was the bearer of a message from God. The message might be a foretelling of some future event, but it didn't have to be. It could be a word to remind people of the truth of God's word and how it applied to their situation at the moment, just like pastors and teachers do today.

A priest had the duty of mediating between God and man. He brought God to the people by teaching the Law, and he brought the people to God by offering sacrifices on their behalf.

A king was to be the leader of the people. When Israel was first formed as a theocracy, God Himself was their king. But when the people asked for a human king, God allowed it but with strict instructions. The king was not to be like the kings of other nations. He was not to multiply wealth and power for himself, but to live as a servant leader of the people. He was not to have many wives as political alliances, because they would lead him astray from God. The king was to have his own copy of the Law and meditate on it day and night to remind himself that he was no better than his people. If he were faithful to the Law, his dynasty would continue in Israel (Deuteronomy 17:14–20).

All three of these roles were anointed by God. When someone officially stepped into one of these leadership roles, a formal ceremony was held. They were anointed with sacred oil, a special recipe given to them by God. But God also anointed His chosen leaders with the Holy Spirit, whether they had been anointed with the sacred oil or not. If they disobeyed, God could take His Holy Spirit away from them, as He did with Saul (1 Samuel 16:14), even they were still the official anointed leader. The word *Messiah* means "anointed one," so it shouldn't have been a surprise that the Messiah would fulfill all three of these roles. Yet the people only expected a king.

When Jesus came on the scene in the New Testament, He fulfilled all three of these anointed roles. He was never officially anointed with sacred oil, but He was God's chosen instrument, anointed with the Holy Spirit in a new way, a way no other person before Him had been. The Holy Spirit didn't just come upon Him, like it had with so many judges and kings before Him. It was even more than being filled with the Spirit like some of the Old Testament leaders had been. Jesus was conceived by the Holy Spirit, so He was by nature both human and divine. Jesus, God's Anointed One, was our ultimate priest, our ultimate prophet, and our ultimate king.

READ JOHN 6:1—15

JESUS, OUR ULTIMATE PROPHET

After Jesus performed the miracle of the feeding of the 5,000, the people declared that He really must be the prophet promised by God. In the Old Testament, prophets empowered by the Holy Spirit often performed miracles to prove that their message really was from God. Jesus did the same. His miracles were so incredible that the people said He must really be from God (John 6:14; 7:30–31). Jesus Himself said to the Jews who opposed Him, "If I am not doing the works of my Father, then do not believe me; but if I do them, even though you do not believe me, believe the works, that you may know and understand that the Father is in me and I am in the Father" (John 10:37–38).

The Jews struggled to believe Jesus's message because it was so different from what they expected. But His miracles were obviously from God. They could not deny that. Some suggested that He got His supernatural powers from demonic forces (John 7:20; 8:48–49). But the works Jesus did were not works of evil; they were works of good. Demonic forces seek to enslave people; Christ's miracles set people free. If Jesus were a demonic force, why would He be casting out demons? (Matthew 12:27). The purpose of His miracles was to declare the good news of the kingdom of God (Luke 4:43). He healed people from disease to show that in the kingdom of God there will be no sickness or pain. He exorcised demons to show that there is no evil in the kingdom of God. He fed the hungry to show there is no hunger or poverty in God's kingdom. He raised the dead to show there will be no death in the kingdom, only eternal life. It was not only the power of His miracles that proved He was a prophet from God; it was the nature of His miracles.

In Deuteronomy, before the people entered the Promised Land, and before they even had a king, Moses promised that the Messiah would be the ultimate prophet. Hearing the voice of God directly and seeing His presence in fire on the mountain was too much for the Israelites to bear, so the Lord promised to raise up a prophet like Moses from among them and put His very words in the prophet's mouth to speak only what God commanded Him (Deuteronomy 18:15–22). God would put His voice and His presence into a person so the people could bear it. Jesus was this ultimate prophet. Because He was God Himself in human form, all of His words were the words of the Father. Jesus Himself said this on more than one occasion: "I do nothing on my own authority but speak just as the Father taught me" (John 8:28; see also John 12:49; 14:10).

Jesus was a different kind of prophet than all who had come before Him. The writer of Hebrews opens the book by saying, "Long ago, at many times and in many ways, God spoke to our fathers by the prophets, but in these last days he has spoken to us by his Son, whom he appointed the heir of all things, through whom he also created the world. He is the radiance of the glory of God and the exact imprint of His nature, and he upholds the universe by the word of his power" (Hebrews 1:1–3). Jesus is greater than a typical prophet because, as the exact expression of God's nature, *everything* He says is a message of God. Jesus spoke only the words of God because He is God. But Jesus is more than just a messenger; He is the image of the invisible God (Colossians 1:15). He doesn't just tell us what God says, Jesus shows us who God is.

This is one of the reasons that Jesus came—so God could show us firsthand what He was like. In Jesus, we see how God handles a tax collector who had been stealing from the people. We see how God deals with religious leaders who nitpicked on the Law but mistreated the people. We see the type of people God chooses as His disciples. We see how God treats the sinners and the outcasts. God had been telling His people who He was for thousands of years. Now He showed them.

If we want to know who God is, then we look at Jesus. If we want to know how God would handle a particular situation, then we look at Jesus. If we want to know what God would say or do, then we look at what Jesus said and did. Jesus is the ultimate Prophet, the ultimate voice of God, because He is God.

QUESTIONS FOR REFLECTION

1. What is the message of Jesus Christ? How would you explain it in your own words?

2. How can you be a prophet—a messenger for Jesus with others?

3. In what ways do we need to change in order to live the way Jesus did?

4. If God speaks through His word, written and preached, how can we hear God's voice in our day-to-day lives?

READ JOHN 1:29; 2:18-21; 17:6-9; AND 19:34-37

JESUS, OUR ULTIMATE PRIEST

The book of Hebrews calls Jesus our great high priest (Hebrews 5–8). The apostle Paul writes that Jesus is the one mediator between God and man (1 Timothy 2:5). But Jesus was not only our ultimate high priest; He was also the ultimate sacrifice and the ultimate temple. We saw in Lesson 3 that because He was God Incarnate, Jesus was the true Passover Lamb who takes away the sins of the world (John 1:29). We saw in Lesson 2 that because the Holy Spirit dwelled in Him in His fullness, Jesus's body was the temple of the Holy Spirit. Jesus is the ultimate High Priest because He offered Himself, the human temple of the Spirit, as the ultimate sacrifice.

The writer of Hebrews explained that in the old covenant, the high priest was required to offer sacrifices year after year. But the sacrifice of Jesus, because He offered His own blood rather than the blood of goats and calves, was a once-for-all sacrifice for all the sins of all people of every time and place (Hebrews 9–10). Hebrews says that the physical temple, the building, was a copy of the heavenly throne room, the true holy place of God. God commanded the people to build the mercy seat of the Ark of the Covenant with two golden cherubim on either side as the place for His presence to dwell, because in heaven, God sits on His throne between two actual cherubim (Exodus 25:10–22; Psalm 80:1; 99:1; Ezekiel 10:1). The temple was the earthly representation of the heavenly reality.

Once a year, the priests of the old covenant entered the earthly representation of the throne room of God, where His presence dwelled, to make atonement for sin. But Jesus, the ultimate high priest, "has entered, not into holy places made with hands, which are copies of the true things, but into heaven itself, now to appear in the presence of God on our behalf" (Hebrews 9:24). The sacrifice of Jesus is eternal because we were redeemed not with perishable things like gold or silver, but with the precious blood of Christ (1 Peter 1:18–19). Therefore, Hebrews explains, "He is the mediator of a new covenant, so that those who are called may receive the promised eternal inheritance" (Hebrews 9:15).

This was a new thing that Jesus did. In the old covenant, only the high priest could enter the Holy of Holies and only once a year. God's presence dwelled with His people, but He was hidden behind the veil of the Holy of Holies. People had to come to the temple to meet with God. In Lesson 8, we learned that in the Incarnation of Jesus, God's presence came down in a person who was literally face-to-face with His people. In Jesus, people didn't have to go to the temple to meet with God. God came to them in Jesus. He came not just to the religious people but to people who otherwise would never have stepped foot in the temple. Jesus was able to go into the messy, dark, and difficult places of our world and meet people where they were.

When Jesus died, the veil of the temple, which separated the Holy of Holies from the people, was torn in two from top to bottom. Jewish tradition says this veil was four inches thick and at least sixty feet high. It could not have been torn with human hands. But when Jesus cried out with a loud voice and gave up His spirit, the veil was torn in two from top to bottom. Access to God was freely available to everyone. Jesus is the mediator of the new covenant, the only way to the Father, because He is the One who tore apart the veil. Now all of us can approach the throne of God with confidence (Hebrews 10:19–20).

QUESTIONS FOR REFLECTION

1. If Jesus is the only mediator between God and humanity, then what is our role in bringing people to God (see 2 Corinthians 5:16–21)?

2. If you think of sharing the gospel as a way to tell others how to be reconciled with God, how does that affect your attitude toward witnessing? Does it make you want to share your faith more, or less? Why?

3. Read Romans 12:1-2 and Hebrews 13:15-16. Since there is no longer a need to offer sacrifices for sin, what kinds of "sacrifices" do we offer to God today?

READ JOHN 1:43-49; 10:1-16; AND 12:12-19

JESUS, OUR ULTIMATE KING

In Mark's Gospel, the first recorded words of Jesus are, "The time is fulfilled, and the kingdom of God is at hand; repent and believe in the gospel" (Mark 1:15). In the book of Luke, when Jesus began His ministry in He told the people, "I must preach the good news of the kingdom of God to the other towns as well; for I was sent for this purpose" (Luke 4:43). This was Jesus's purpose, to usher in the kingdom of God. Because Jesus is the true King.

Jesus was the One they had been waiting for. The One they had been longing for. But He wasn't exactly what they were expecting. They misunderstood the promises about the Messiah because they were putting their hopes in the wrong kind of leader. They were looking for a conquering hero—which Jesus was, but not in the way they expected. They were thinking far too small.

What the people of Jesus's day didn't understand was that God's new covenant isn't about a physical temple or an earthly kingdom. Jesus's kingdom was bigger than that. Jesus came to build a kingdom that was "not of this world" (John 18:36) and a temple in the heart of every believer (1 Corinthians 3:16). Understanding this tension explains why so many people rejected Jesus's message and why the reactions of the crowds on Palm Sunday didn't bring Jesus joy but reduced Him to tears (Luke 19:41–44).

It is in Jesus's triumphal entry on Palm Sunday that we most clearly see the tension between what the people wanted Jesus to be and who He really was. The way Jesus chose to enter Jerusalem proclaimed two almost paradoxical things. First, He was definitely declaring that He was the Messiah. Riding on a donkey intentionally fulfilled the Messianic prophecy of Zechariah 9:9. At the same time, the triumphal entry showed the crowds what *kind* of king He was. And it was not the norm.

In the Roman Empire, a triumphal procession of a military leader celebrated his recent victory. He would ride through the city on his war horse or in a chariot, draped in a royal tunic, holding a laurel branch in right hand and an ivory scepter in his left. A parade of priests, musicians, members of the Senate, and an army of soldiers would follow him. Prisoners of war and spoil from the battle were also paraded through the streets to show off his victory.

Jesus didn't come charging in on a war horse or a chariot, but on an animal associated with peace. A donkey was humble and used for civil rather than military processions. Compared to a Roman procession, Jesus's "triumphal entry" was almost laughable. It was nowhere near as grand, with only a small crowd of people, none of whom was important. And He hadn't actually won any battles yet, so their cheering was more in anticipation of his becoming a military hero. They were looking ahead to a victory they believed He would bring, not one He had already accomplished.

The people's response was appropriate—calling Him King, recognizing that He came in the name of the Lord, asking Him to save them, calling for peace. Yet they still misunderstood what kind of king He was. His was a peace gained not through war, but through death and sacrifice. He would save them, but not from Rome. His victory would be greater than any physical battle. He would overcome sin and death itself.

This is exactly the kind of king Zechariah described, "humble and riding on a donkey" (Zechariah 9:9), yet they still expected Him to be like the conquering Roman heroes. Jesus had made it clear what kind of king He was, and it was exactly the image God used for Himself in the Old Testament—the Good Shepherd (John 10:1–16). In Ezekiel, God described the wicked kings of Israel who, as bad shepherds, used the people for their own gain, not giving but taking from their flocks. They didn't strengthen the weak, heal the sick, bind up the injured, or search for the lost (Ezekiel 34:1–10). Jeremiah and Zechariah also had scathing words for the bad shepherds. "Woe to the shepherds who destroy and scatter the sheep of my pasture!" (Jeremiah 23:1). "Woe to the worthless shepherd who deserts the flock" (Zechariah 11:17).

But God is a Good Shepherd who tends his flock gently, provides for all their needs, gives them rest, guides them in the right way, keeps them safe, and cares for them through difficult times (Isaiah 40:11; Psalm 23). So, too, Jesus is that Good Shepherd. The king who cares for His sheep as tenderly and intimately as a shepherd does His flock. The king knows each of his sheep individually. They hear His voice and follow it (John 10:1–16). He is the king who would leave His whole flock to go searching for one who was lost (Luke 15:1–7). A servant king who does not use the sheep for His own gain but, ultimately, lays down His life for His sheep. Jesus uses the phrase "lay down my life" five times in just eight verses (John 10:10–8).

Instead of a conquering hero, Jesus was a servant king. The king who "did not count equality with God a thing to be grasped but emptied himself by taking the form of a servant . . . [and] humbled himself by becoming obedient to the point of death, even death on a cross" (Philippians 2:6–8). Jesus was the Son of Man, the divine king. And yet "the Son of Man came not to be served but to serve, and to give His life as a ransom for many" (Matthew 20:28).

Every quality they expected in a king—might, strength, power—is true of Jesus, but not in the way they imagined. His strength was shown in sacrifice, His love in washing feet. His power was used not to overthrow Rome but to overcome sin, disease, evil, and death. He never sat on an earthly throne and he wore only a crown of thorns. He only ever fought spiritual battles. But when His mission was over, God highly exalted Him, "so that at the name of Jesus every knee should bow, in heaven and on earth and under the earth, and every tongue confess that Jesus Christ is Lord, to the glory of God the Father" (Philippians 2:10–11).

QUESTIONS FOR REFLECTION

1. In what areas do you struggle to honor Jesus as King? In what ways do you try to put yourself on the throne instead?

2. What's one thing you can start doing or change right now to honor Jesus as King over your life?

3. Why is it important to see Jesus as Prophet, Priest, and King? What happens when we fail to see Him in one or more of these roles?

RESOURCES

Beasley-Murray, George R. *John*. Word Biblical Commentary. Dallas: Word, 1987.

Blum, Edwin. *The Bible Knowledge Commentary: New Testament*. Colorado Springs: David C. Cook, 1983.

Brown, Raymond. *The Gospel and Epistles of John: A Concise Commentary*. Collegeville, MN: Liturgical Press, 1988.

Burney, C. F. *The Aramaic Origin of the Fourth Gospel*. Oxford: Clarendon Press, 1922.

Horton, Michael. *The Christian Faith: A Systematic Theology for Pilgrims on the Way*. Grand Rapids: Zondervan, 2011.

Josephus. *Vita: The Life of Flavius Josephus*. Auckland: The Floating Press, 2008, http://www.sacred-texts.com/jud/josephus/autobiog.html.

Keener, Craig S. *The IVP Bible Background Commentary: New Testament*. Downers Grove, IL: InterVarsity Press, 1993.

Klett, Fred. "Sukkot: A Promise of Living Water." *Jews for Jesus*. http://jewsforjesus.org/publications/issues/v06-n07/sukkot.

Kohler, Kaufmann. "Wisdom." *The Jewish Encyclopedia*. New York: Funk & Wagnalls, 1906.

Kummel, Werner G. *Theology of the New Testament*. London: SCM Press, 1976.

Lewis, C. S. *Mere Christianity*. New York: Macmillan / Collier, 1952.

Lindsley, Art. "Argument from Agape." *Knowing and Doing*. C. S. Lewis Institute, 2007.

Morris, Leon. *The Gospel According to John*. Grand Rapids: Eerdmans, 1971.

Pritchard, Ray. "Samaria: The Place Jesus Must Visit." *Crosswalk*, March 13, 2012. http://www.crosswalk.com/blogs/dr-ray-pritchard/samaria-the-place-jesus-must-visit.html.

Ridderbos, Herman N. *The Gospel According to John: A Theological Commentary*. Grand Rapids: Eerdmans, 1997.

Sproul, R.C. *John: St. Andrew's Expositional Commentary*. Lake Mary, FL: Reformation Trust, 2009.

Stott, John. *Basic Christianity*. Downers Grove, IL: Intervarsity Press, 2008.

Vander Laan, Ray. "The Jewish Revolts." *In the Dust of the Rabbi, That the World May Know*. Vol. 6. Grand Rapids: Zondervan, 2006.

Warnock, Adrian. *Raised with Christ: How the Resurrection Changes Everything*. Wheaton, IL: Crossway, 2009.

Wright, Christopher J. H. *Knowing Jesus through the Old Testament*. Downers Grove, IL: IVP Academic, 2014.

Made in USA - Kendallville, IN
1124276_9781703695229
06.16.2020 0812